*Studies in Writing & Rhetoric*

## Other Books in the Studies in Writing & Rhetoric Series

*Sexuality and the Politics of Ethos
in the Writing Classroom*

# Sexuality and the Politics of Ethos in the Writing Classroom

Zan Meyer Gonçalves

SOUTHERN ILLINOIS UNIVERSITY PRESS

*Carbondale*

Copyright © 2005 by The Conference on College Composition and
Communication of the National Council of Teachers of English
All rights reserved
Printed in the United States of America
08  07  06  05   4  3  2  1

Publication partially funded by a subvention grant from The Conference on College
Composition and Communication of the National Council of Teachers of English.

*Library of Congress Cataloging-in-Publication Data*
Gonçalves, Zan Meyer, 1962–
   Sexuality and the politics of ethos in the writing classroom / Zan Meyer
Gonçalves.
       p. cm. — (Studies in writing & rhetoric)
   Includes bibliographical references and index.
     1. English language—Rhetoric—Study and teaching—Psychological aspects. 2.
English language—Rhetoric—Study and teaching—Social aspects. 3. Report
writing—Study and teaching (Higher). 4. Sexual orientation—Social aspects. 5.
Transsexuals—Education (Higher). 6. Bisexuals—Education (Higher). 7. Homo-
sexuality and education. 8. Gays—Education (Higher). 9. Identity (Psychology).
10. Group identity. I. Title. II. Series.
PE1404.G643 2005
808'.042'071—dc22
ISBN 0-8093-2676-0 (pbk. : alk. paper)       2005015421

Printed on recycled paper. ♻

The paper used in this publication meets the minimum requirements of American
National Standard for Information Sciences—Permanence of Paper for Printed
Library Materials, ANSI Z39.48-1992. ∞

*To Bob and Isabel, my first writing teachers*

# Contents

# Preface

Dear Zan,

At the beginning of the semester I really did "suck" at writing. Okay, fine. I didn't suck but I didn't feel very comfortable with where I was as a writer. . . . I often find myself either writing something totally different than what I was thinking, or I would ramble. . . . I went from saying goofy, 11th grade sentences to saying something like "This decision was detrimental on many levels, it not only alienated a young woman and her family from the town her family built . . ." I felt as the semester went on, I could see me change as a writer. My sentences were strong and full where as before they were wimpy, almost nonexistent. I would like to thank you Zan . . . for what you did in the classroom. You made my freshman year a challenge on many levels, but a good challenge :-).

T. J. Debbs

**A** composition teacher's fantasy. That's what T. J. Debbs's in-class final for first-year college writing was. As I read T. J.'s reflective essay describing his work as a writer over the course of the semester, I was pleased to see he had learned a good deal about audience and persuasion. In this excerpt, T. J. constructs a rhetorical self that is at first an outsider, an outsider who becomes an insider to a community of writers. He also invites me, his writing instructor, into the role of valued mentor and fellow writer. The ethos T. J. performs in this piece reflects a complex blend of several identities: a writer comfortable with using the vernacular and slang; a literary critic able to reflect on a published text; an academic able to comment specifically on how his writing had changed, supporting his claim with a concrete example from his own work; and a person able to evaluate his own growth. The identities T. J. performs more or less successfully are a far cry from the role of "student" as passive recipient of information. The role of "student," according to Linda Brodkey, Robert Brooke, and many other composition scholars, is the role most often offered by educational discourse, a role many of us believe is antithetical to becoming a writer. In the field of composition, we often pride ourselves on offering a pedagogy that invites rhetorical growth, encouraging students to think for themselves and recognize themselves as writers and even citizens, active participants in their own education and communities.

Those of us who teach writing have continued to challenge one another on how to best facilitate rhetorical growth for all students in our first-year composition classes. In particular, we have puzzled over how the social identities of the writers in our classrooms influence their writing and their ability to write, seriously questioning our role as composition teachers regarding social activism and identity politics. We have wondered how to address the identity-writing issue in terms of pedagogy and whether teaching writing grounded in identity—in writing assignments that focus on what is personally important to writers—will lead to rhetorical growth or to self-absorbed, "confessional" writing. And then there is the problem of how to ensure that the rhetorical growth writers achieve in the first-year composition classroom will transfer to writing success in another context.

In this book, I invite teachers of composition to reconsider the importance of ethos in addressing these conundrums. I ask that we focus our attention on ethos by noting how writers and speakers regularly craft identity performances for rhetorical effect and to understand how those identity performances are shaped by the complex and often inequitable social contexts of our classrooms and communities. I aim to offer a new way of thinking about ethos, an approach grounded in classical ethos, identity performance, specificity, and intersectionality. As we develop this particular lens for ethos, I hope to illustrate the following in relation to the issues above:

- Define the relationship between a writer's social identities and what and how he or she writes by considering identity as a series of multiple and in-flux performances shaped, though not wholly determined, by social discourses.

- Discuss the place of social activism and identity politics in the composition classroom by inviting students to consider their social identities and the "truths" they believe as a function of social discourses rather than transcendental discourses.
- Assist writers to make transfers across rhetorical contexts by teaching students this new definition of ethos as context-bound identity performances.
- Encourage students to locate their personal passions and guide writers to link those interests to public conversations by providing a space where students can name the competing "truths" from both subjugated and dominant discourses.

This book also presents an opportunity to learn directly from the experience of those who claim a gay, lesbian, bisexual, and/or transgendered (GLBT) identity. The social justice wing of composition studies has advocated, and rightly so, for teachers to learn enough about GLBT students' concerns to create some sense of safety for them in what is still a homophobic culture. This book shows how GLBT writers are already engaged in creating that safety for themselves through the sophisticated work of rhetorical identity constructions. Queer theory and practice provide a way to articulate that work and to rethink the importance of "ethos" as a primary site for rhetorical work and learning.

The undergraduate students described in this book came from a variety of backgrounds. The one thing they had in common was their desire to address homophobia and heterosexism on campus. These students were part of the Speaker's Bureau of the Stonewall Center: a GLBT resource center at the University of Massachusetts at Amherst. The Bureau is an educational outreach program of the Stonewall Center; the purpose of the Bureau is to educate the campus and surrounding community about the lives of those who identify as non-heterosexual in an effort to combat homophobia and heterosexism. On campus, student speakers are invited by instructors and resident advisers to address these issues with their peers.

Typically, panels of two to five speakers tell their stories to audiences and then open the floor for dialogue with an audience about "controversial issues that are usually only discussed in the absence of those whose lives are being questioned." The guiding philosophy of the Bureau encourages its members to "honor the vulnerability of [their and others'] lived experience" and to invite audience members to do the same and in particular "to disclose and examine their own fears and/or intolerance" (*Speaker's Bureau Manual* 2). Student speakers begin in Bureau workshops designed to help them select what parts of their lived experiences they will story for their peers and for what purpose.

This is not a new experience for these students. Most of the students who come to the Bureau to speak do so because they are tired of storying their lived experiences in a way that "reads" as heterosexual for their peers. They have for years been editing and hiding those parts of their lived experiences that fall outside the dominant story that heterosexism tells about women and men, and they have been performing identities considered "legal" for "real" women and men. It is a desire to claim a positive "gay" social identity and create an environment that will support that identity that propels these students to become speakers on the Bureau. These speakers are intent on repositioning themselves as more than simply "gay" and on creating and performing a positive, complicated, and human social identity for themselves as "gay."

Like the students in our first-year composition classes, the students in this book came from various cities, small and large, industrial and suburban, and identify in a variety of ways, including differing class backgrounds and other identifiers, and like the students in our classes, they also shared a common university community. The students in this book attended the University of Massachusetts at Amherst, a large public research university set in a rural and progressive area that accommodates several small private liberal arts colleges as well. During the time of the study upon which this book is based, there were 17,000 undergraduates and 6,000 graduates enrolled (these and the statistics that follow were taken from *Student Affairs Research,* by UMass at Amherst Center for Institutional Research). The student body supported a wide variety of student organizations ranging from Campus Crusade for Christ and the Republican Club to the Cannabis Coalition and the Radical Student Union as well as many clubs based on racial/ethnic identity or hobbies. Despite the variety of student organizations, the undergraduate student body was fairly homogeneous: predominantly white (80 percent) and young (18–22 years) with a history of tensions around issues of race/ethnicity, gender, and sexual identity manifested as assault, harassment, bigotry, and stereotyping. In one survey, 58 percent of respondents felt that anti-gay/lesbian/bisexual attitudes existed on campus to "some" extent and 27 percent to a "great" or "very great" extent with 30 percent reporting that they had witnessed stereotyping or negative remarks or harassment. Men were twice as likely to report that they would "do nothing" if they witnessed harassing behavior (40 percent for men compared to 21 percent for women). The picture for gender-based and racial/ethnic harassment is similar. In regard to having experienced stereotyping by other students, African Americans reported 78 percent, Latinos 88 percent, Asians 73 percent, and whites 62 percent. (See *Project Pulse,* by UMass at Amherst Center for Institutional Research, for more information on these surveys.)

The students represented in this book lived their academic lives amidst these tensions and faced them directly in many of their classes, at the forums at which they spoke, and at the social events they attended at the university. It is primarily through the experiences of five students—Vincente Colon, Sulli Schwartz, Viany Rivera, Jamar Evans, and Moe Pontiack—that I hope to show how they learned to use the texts of their lived experiences in order to construct and perform a complex public ethos.[1] I will show in the following chapters how the focal student speakers and other student speakers used the training they received on the Bureau to perform specific identities in order to persuade their audiences to become allies.

I am advocating a pedagogy based on what I have learned about ethos from the student speakers on the Speaker's Bureau, as identity performances bound by social discourses. I encourage you as writers and teachers of writing to consider this praxis, one of a few that invites students to make sense of themselves, the world, and their place in it. My experience has shown me that, more often than not, this new way of looking at ethos as specific identity performance can

guide students to build a bridge between the personal and the public. In the process, I have seen students contribute valuable strategies in order to address pressing social dilemmas in the multiple
communities to which we all belong.

# Acknowledgments

First and foremost, I want to thank the students and fellow activists, those people who shared their writing, speaking, and thinking with me. Your stories continue to move me and instruct me. I think of you all often and with much gratitude.

Second, I want to thank a series of very fine mentors, the most recent being Robert Brooke, the editor of this series, and Christine Stewart-Nuñez, the assistant editor. They together have provided the impetus for me to draft and redraft this manuscript into the actual book it has become. I am particularly indebted to Robert for teaching me how I might frame my chapters as arguments rather than as solely narrative and to Christine for more than a few crucial framing ideas as well as brilliant chapter titles and subtitles. Thank you both for your patience and encouragement.

And to those who assisted me in the final editing process—Isabel Meyer, Sharon Kennedy, Julie Bush, and Carol Burns—a huge thank you.

I am particularly grateful for those who mentored me at the University of Massachusetts at Amherst: Anne Herrington, Charlie Moran, Judith Solsken, Marcia Curtis, Irene Price, Heidi Terault, Peter Elbow, and Deb Carlin. I would not have persevered through the doctoral program if not for these people and my graduate program cohorts, in particular Paul Puccio, Tom Deans, Andrea Stover, Kim Costino, Nika Hogan, Mya Poe, Nancy Cheever, Mike Mattison, and Missy Marie Montgomery. Thank you all for your generosity and humor.

Never would I have imagined that I would leave California to pursue a doctorate if not for Judith Rodby, Thia Wolf, and most especially Tom Fox, who was absolutely certain I needed to pursue my studies further in Massachusetts.

My nonacademic community has been equally important to me in this endeavor. Without the support of spiritual groups like the

I-Opener, Attitude Adjustments, and Saturday Morning Group as well as the Nonviolent Communication Group, none of this would be possible. I thank the following fellow beings for feeding, housing, and loving me through this last stretch: Bob and Isabel Meyer, Nick and Colleen Nicholas, Mimi Erceg and Susan Fisher, Kayla and Coni, Rita Beier, Sheila and Cole Rhodes-Dow, Christine J. and Vinnie Cifelli, Patty Barr and Kay Monroe, Beth Moore and Rebecca Kennet, Gene and Cheri and Zephyr Monette, Rebecca Jackson and Ted Giles, Tom Murray and Victoria Yoshen, and Sahse and Little Bit. If I were truly to list all my "twenty best friends" it would take much more space, so I'll just add a few more: the Donovans, Rachel and Sharon, Sum, Kate, Martha, Lorraine, Bill, Abbey and Liisa, Chris and Beta and Nick and Tina Meyer, Lynn Werthhamer, Joni Doherty, Donna Reck, Nancy and Chey, Anne Stork, Nick Lupinin, Don Farrelly and Phil Shinnick, Laura and Yano Porter, and Molly and Michael Haas; and those who went before: Maria and Joe and Carl Gonçalves, Virginia Garrett, and George Washington Rhodes-Dow; and last, those from whom I learned much about compassion: Kimberly, Lisa, Rebecca, and Shirley.

*Sexuality and the Politics of Ethos
in the Writing Classroom*

# 1 / Performing Identities/Performing Social Change

> I loved walking in there and just watching the reactions on their faces. Some of the girls were like, "No, get out of here!" And this and that. And the guys would be like, "That dude's gay?" And it totally breaks down to what they think gay people are supposed to be like . . . or look like. . . . I want to let people know that gay people are . . . some gay people are down-to-earth, not so far from you . . . a lot more than you think. I've done a lot of Speaker's Bureaus, and if I somehow changed . . . someone's view on gay people, maybe like five people, it's so worth it.

**V**incente Colon looked directly into my eyes as he spoke, occasionally smiling broadly and finally nodding emphatically as he finished answering my question. When I met Vincente, it was his first year as a student speaker for the Speaker's Bureau, a university-based educational outreach program designed to address homophobia and heterosexism on campus and in the community. Vincente's facility at gauging particular audiences and creating a variety of multiple and shifting identities or subject positions to address those audiences was a commonplace ability on the Bureau among both undergraduate and graduate speakers.

The excerpt above is from an interview I had with Vincente when I was gathering information for my ethnographic study of Speaker's Bureau literacy practices and was also a fellow speaker with Vincente on the Bureau. At that time, Vincente was a twenty-year-old junior who identified as gay, Puerto Rican, and a dancer. I had asked Vincente in this interview to tell me about any particularly satisfying presentations he had done for the Bureau. Below is an excerpt of the story he told at one presentation.

1

I'm Vincente, I'm a junior. This is my first Speaker's Bureau. I've always known. I remember being six years old and attracted to boys. How many people enjoyed junior high? No one? Maybe a few. Everyone always teases. When I was younger, I had feminine characteristics. Once my friends were playing around with a makeup compact, so I played with it too, pretending to put makeup on. These four guys came around the corner and said, "You faggot!" That was an awful experience.

Though an undergraduate, Vincente's answer and story spoke of a kind of rhetorical sophistication I rarely saw in the undergraduate students I had been teaching in the writing classroom. How, I wondered, did Vincente and the others on the Bureau learn to manage the rhetorical triangle with such finesse? And Vincente and the others often did so with frankly hostile audiences who regularly commented in post-presentation evaluations that they were surprised, for example, that they liked Vincente and admired his courage, as they had always considered gay men "weird and disgusting" and "didn't know Puerto Ricans could be gay."

I also began to wonder about the unique situation of the Bureau: in what ways was it different from the writing and speaking situation in our writing classrooms, and how did those differences contribute to the sort of attention to ethos, purpose, and audience I saw in Vincente's and the others' speaking and writing? It seemed to me that unlike many of the students I taught, Vincente and the other speakers had learned that composing—either for speaking or writing—is about making a series of choices, creating rhetorical constructions of themselves in a variety of contexts for a variety of purposes and audiences. It became clear to me as I studied the literacy practices of the Speaker's Bureau that the experience of speaking for the Bureau apparently enabled the student speakers to work against rhetorical constructions of gay people that are stigmatized. As they did so, they interrupted and challenged these constructions and offered new constructions of themselves.

In the excerpt above, we can see Vincente not only working against the dominant, homophobic rhetorical construction of himself as "gay" but also offering a new rhetorical construction of himself as a proud "gay man." Vincente performed his identity among competing discourses, creating an ethos that simultaneously appealed to and shaped his audience. Vincente clearly spoke to the preconceived notions his audience held. In the classical rhetorical tradition, Vincente offered his audience members roles to play. He created roles or new subject positions for his listeners by first inviting them to see themselves as "not so far" from him and then as allies who hold a new positive view about "gay people." Vincente knew from repeated readings of his peers what "they think gay people are supposed to be like." In response, he offered a counter-discourse, an outlaw discourse from which he created a "down-to-earth," positive role or ethos for himself in order to persuade his audiences that homophobia is unnecessary.

The influence of a writer's identities on his or her writing and ability to learn to write has been the topic of much discussion in the field of composition. Many see college writing as a context that requires students to create and inhabit a new identity and experience a concomitant loss of an old identity. Others see the issue of identity and writing as inexorably bound to social inequities around gender/race/class/sexuality/disability and call for teachers of writing to address identity politics in their classrooms.

In this chapter, I offer a new way to approach the influence of students' identities on their writing and ability to learn to write. I propose that we directly address identity and the ways in which we who teach in the first-year writing classroom acknowledge identity issues and identity-based social inequities. In this book, I ask us to consider teaching the students in our first-year composition classes to become aware of the multiple identities they inhabit and the new identities they may need to construct in college. I suggest we create opportunities in our classrooms for students to examine the beliefs they hold, the beliefs that through language maintain, reproduce, resist, or transform social inequities based on identity. In this way, we can teach all of our students to see the utility of thinking about identity as a performance, as a rhetorical engagement with their social location and their target audience.

Central to this new approach is my idea of specific identity performance, a redefinition and reclamation of ethos as possibly the most important site of rhetorical work and learning. I suggest we teach students that they can invite audiences to become allies around issues important to them and move those people to action. We can teach students to "get specific" and draw on their lived experiences and choose how they construct and perform a variety of specific identities to persuade audiences. We can create opportunities for students to see how their agency or autonomy is necessarily bound by the discourses, the cultural norms and "truths," that define their concepts of the world, one another, and themselves. The main goal, then, is to teach students to think critically about identity construction and performance, then to ground that understanding in their social context. Doing so will encourage students to analyze and deconstruct cultural claims, norms, and "truths" as texts and in turn to analyze and deconstruct claims in any kind of text—including academic arguments. In the process, we can show students how to connect their personal needs—for acceptance, contribution, and integrity—to the public realm.

When we as teachers acknowledge that our students inhabit multiple identities, we can invite them to become conscious and aware of these multiple identities and the social forces that shape their performances of ethos. By doing so, student writers are in a better position to choose how to best perform their ethos in order to connect with and move audiences.

In this book, I invite readers to learn from the experience of student speakers on the Speaker's Bureau and the structure that the Bureau employs to guide undergraduate student speakers, like Vincente, to consciously choose which identities to perform (how, for whom, and for what purpose). Student speakers on the Bureau learn to address their audiences, to connect with their peers first by acknowledging who their audience is and then by invoking the audience they want their peers to be. The speakers want their peers to be capable of resisting homophobia and countering heterosexism.

The ethos student speakers perform encourages their audiences to analyze and deconstruct heterosexist "truths" and offers a new set of outlaw "truths," a set that supports and celebrates a variety of sexual and gender identities outside of compulsory heterosexuality and rigidly polarized roles for "real" men and women.

Throughout this book, I will return again and again to examine the way student speakers on the Bureau are always already engaged in the rhetorical work of specific identity performance. I will use the experience of student speakers as writers and speakers to better understand how we might assist all students in our classrooms to more successfully use specific identity performances in their writing and become aware of the rhetorical choices they make as they construct ethos.

In some ways, the new perspective on ethos I am offering in this book is not so far from what compositionists Lisa Ede and Andrea Lunsford note that successful writers have. One of the components of ethos I focus on is the ability of a writer to move between addressing and invoking an audience. In their article on audience, Ede and Lunsford use an example of a student who writes to her neighbors proposing that they accept and support the relocation of a halfway house in their neighborhood. The writer in Ede and Lunsford's article begins as Vincente did, by recognizing and addressing her very real audience directly, choosing particular things that she and they know about themselves—for example, their generosity and fairness. And again, like Vincente, she invokes the audience she wants them to be by selecting particular roles or subject positions she wants her neighbors to assume, encouraging them to take up the position of open-minded people concerned with the well-being of those to occupy the halfway house. She too attends to her ethos, positioning herself as believable and trustworthy. She creates this rhetorical construction of herself by choosing to tell particular stories about herself from her own lived experience that will appeal to and hence position and move her audience. All these choices serve her purpose, to persuade her audience that, in this case, it is unnecessary to fear the relocation of the halfway house in their neighborhood.

As I interviewed, worked with, and observed Vincente and the other undergraduate student speakers and writers in this book, I began to develop a new frame of reference for understanding the rhetorical situation of the writing classroom. I noted that, unlike the situation in many writing classrooms, the Bureau performed three important functions:

- It positioned student speakers as experts and educators.
- It offered student speakers new ways to read their own private, lived experiences as important texts necessarily connected to the public sphere.
- It guided students to create ethos by selecting, shaping, and revising the texts of their lived experiences into multiple "true" stories about themselves in which they developed and performed a variety of identities in order to connect with and move their audiences.

These components apparently assist student speakers to create positive new social identities for themselves and thus affect the whole social framework they and their peers inhabit.

As I began to apply to my own first-year writing classes what I was learning about the Bureau, I clearly saw it was possible to teach my students how they too could choose to see their identities as multiple, specific, and performative and use this knowledge to connect to and move audiences. This was an important discovery for me. Like many writing teachers, I had puzzled over how to invite undergraduates to write narratives based on their lived experiences and how to guide students to connect these private experiences to a public discourse. What I learned from the student speakers and the Bureau was how I might craft a curriculum to guide students to see the connection between selecting and revising "true" stories about themselves and moving an audience. I began to develop a curriculum that guided students to create an ethos based on multiple and specific performances of identities. I saw that the structure of the Bureau, adapted to the writing classroom, could assist students in successfully speaking and writing within and across a variety of discourses, including academic discourses. (I saw this in the school writing samples the student speakers in this study gave me, particularly when they referenced their experiences as gay, lesbian, bisexual, or transgendered people.)

The aim of this book is to provide examples of how we can adapt the functions that the Bureau performs for students to our own classrooms and use the experiences of the student speakers to guide us. Each chapter contains examples of specific identity performances that student speakers on the Bureau "do" in their interviews with me, in their panel presentations to classes, on their Web sites and in letters to the editor, or in their writing for classes and exams. It is my hope that these examples will enable us to shape a pedagogy that can assist our own first-year writing students to understand the choices they make as writers among competing discourses and in particular the function of ethos in moving audiences both inside and outside the classroom. This chapter begins to answer the question of how we as teachers can use the writing classroom to assist all students in identifying issues of rhetorical identity construction in relation to audience as well as to competing social discourses—an ability that is important, even necessary for those students who identify as GLBT.

The remaining sections of this chapter provide a context for this work and highlight and explain my redefinition of ethos as specific identity performance: a synthesis of identity performance theory, a theory of specificity, intersectionality, and the classical definition of ethos.

*Establishing a Complicated Ethos*

I came to a new definition of ethos as specific identity performance by reflecting on three theories: Judith Butler's identity performance theory, political theorist Shane Phelan's theory of specificity, and the theory of intersectionality as it emerges from queer theory. I add to these theories Anne Herrington and Marcia Curtis's idea of a "sponsoring institution" as well as William P. Banks's idea of embodied writing. I begin this section with a review of the classical use of ethos as a rhetorical strategy and then introduce how I am using Butler, Phelan, and intersectionality as well as the ideas of sponsoring institutions and embodied writing to understand what it is student speakers are learning and doing on the Bureau as speakers, inside the classroom as students, and outside the classroom as citizens.

Vincente and the other participants on the Bureau have learned to construct and perform their identities in order to move a variety of audiences. Essentially, student speakers use what Aristotle and rhetoricians of his time thought of as ethos—the creation of personas that appear to possess and are regarded as possessing genuine wisdom and excellence of character—in order to persuade their audiences. The construction of character in order to appeal to audiences is one of the means of persuasion in any rhetorical situation. Cicero speaks of shaping and moving audiences by using ethos to offer up positions for audience members to play. Modern rhetoricians also point to the role of ethos in persuasion. Kenneth Burke discusses in great detail the central importance of ethos to his project of creating "identification" between speakers/writers and their audiences. Thomas Newkirk, a current compositionist, does not explicitly refer to ethos or the concept of Burkean identification in his book *The Performance of Self in Student Writing;* however, he aptly describes what happens when Burkean identification does not happen. Newkirk notes that the "selves" students construct in their essays most often reflect an audience who values romantic, sentimental, pastoral, or confessional genres, not an academic English department audience who values modern and postmodern literary genres. In the process, students lose their academic audience, and academics dismiss, or perhaps simply miss, the selves, the ethos, students do create.

These rhetorical constructions place the focus on the rhetor's agency and do not consider how social discourses constrain this agency. Vincente's construction of rhetorical identity—as is the case with perhaps most speakers and writers who identify as GLBT— wasn't simply a function of agency but also a function of response to the normative social discourses that inscribe "gayness" with a language of exclusion and othering.

Judith Butler's theory of identity performance can help us to better understand what it is speakers on the Bureau are doing in relation to these social discourses. One of the tenets of Butler's theory is that we construct and perform our various rhetorical identities intentionally as a survival strategy within social discourses that essentially determine and govern that performance (139). Vincente's intentional rhetorical constructions and performances of himself on the Bureau were a survival strategy located within what Butler describes as discourses of compulsory heterosexuality and gender hierarchy. These discourses determine both legal and outlaw identity performances (87). Compulsory heterosexuality defines heterosexuality as the only "true" or legal expression of sexuality, outlawing other expressions. Gender hierarchy positions those identified as male as more valuable than those who are identified as female, outlawing performances that suggest otherwise or blur the distinction between "real" men and women. According to these social discourses, to act as a gay man is to participate in a "false" or "illegal" expression of sexuality and gender that in turn upsets the gender hierarchy. The gender hierarchy holds that "real" men choose women as partners; a man choosing a man as a partner is a performance that suggests there may not be a "natural" gender hierarchy. When Vincente constructed himself as "down-to-earth" and "gay," he signaled a different, outlaw discourse within which he could exist as both "real" and "legal."

The Speaker's Bureau offers a unique place for Vincente and other speakers to create, revise, and maintain a counter-, outlaw discourse about sexual difference that in turn inscribes "gayness" with a language of inclusion and value. The students in our own classrooms also function within social discourses that limit and define the kinds of identity performances that are "legal." Ideologies such as sexism, racism, classism, ablism, and heterosexism (and other oppressive identity-based ideologies) all influence the types of identity performances the students in our classrooms create. Students who understand that each of us creates a variety of identities within the constraints of many competing social discourses can better exercise their agency to make choices in relation to creating ethos and persuading their audiences.

Identity performance theory can help us as teachers of writing to understand the limited usefulness of the notion that identity is fixed and unitary and can help us to introduce instead identity as a contingent performance shaped by context as much as by the agency of any one rhetor. The idea that social discourses govern and determine rhetorical constructions of identity does not mean that individuals cannot assert their agency to create identity performances that contest the "truths" asserted by normative social discourses; as Butler says, we need not be "trapped within the unnecessary binarism of free will and determinism. Construction is not opposed to agency; it is the necessary scene of agency" (147). In other words, though we cannot get outside of or avoid the situation of being constructed by discourses, the multiple and competing nature of these discourses creates spaces to develop an awareness, a critical perspective, that in turn makes room for individual rhetors to make some choices and thus exert agency.

Vincente and his fellow undergraduate speakers on the Bureau use their agency and this space to contest the "truths" embedded in the normative social discourses that offer stigmatized positions for "gay" people. In the example at the beginning of this chapter, Vincente is using an outlaw discourse that defines "gay" in a way different from his audience's definition. When Vincente reports, "The guys would be like, 'That dude's *gay*?'" and then says, "Some *gay* people are down-to-earth," I have a clear sense that there are two conflicting "truths" or definitions about what it means to be gay. This is an example of what Butler calls "strategies of subversive repetition" used to contest the normative discourses' constructions, in this case, of "gay" people (147). In the following chapter, I'll show how speakers on Bureau panel presentations use subversive repetition to repeat jokes about "gay people" in a way that redefines those jokes as homophobic rather than funny.

In the process of creating new, outlaw identity performances and naming the conflicting "truths" about gay people, some speakers construct a new fixed and unitary "gay" identity with its own exclusions and othering. Because the Bureau is an identity-based group, it is "within the framework of identity politics," noted Felice Yeskel, the director of the Stonewall Center (the GLBT resource center where the Bureau is housed), in our interview. Identity politics encourages the performance of identity as fixed, unitary, and essential. According to Yeskel, though identity politics has been "important and very useful," she and Bureau speakers see how identity politics as a strategy can be counterproductive, not the most effective means of persuading audiences that homophobia is unnecessary.

When speakers conceive of identity as essential, fixed, and unitary, they often create an identity performance that reproduces exclusive definitions of who gay people are or can be. In the process, speakers inadvertently reproduce hierarchies based on differences both within the "gay" community and between themselves and their audiences. For example, if speakers define "good gays" as those who are "out of the closet" advocating "gay rights" and who appear to follow gender role norms congruent with their biological sex in all but their choice of partner, then those who do not meet this definition are effectively restigmatized.[2] These exclusive definitions in turn define who is "really" an ally based on sameness of identity, leaving those who do not share the same identity as untrustworthy others. Identity politics can, as Yeskel noted, lead speakers into "giving up on all heterosexual people as the enemy" and restigmatizing and dismissing as allies those "gay" or transgendered people who don't follow gender and other dominant norms.

Yeskel and others on the Bureau have sought to address the limits of what I have come to see as the sort of ethos invited by the discourse of identity politics in three ways:

- asking speakers to speak only for themselves, not all "gay people"
- encouraging speakers to name and claim their own multiple identities and the process of how they have come to claim these identities
- adding heterosexual allies to the Bureau

These strategies introduce a discourse based on coalition politics rather than identity politics. The discourse of coalition politics in turn offers speakers a new position from which to perform their identities. As Yeskel aptly described the shift, "In political terms maybe I would say [this new perspective] is a belief that allies are possible and a desire to make them." Encouraging speakers to present their identities as multiple, in process, and shifting and to foreground an agreement or identification around issues instead of around identity opens up a space where speakers can more effectively invite audiences who inhabit a variety of identities to become allies.

In order to better understand how student speakers use identity performance to engage in social action and make allies, I turned to political theorist Shane Phelan's book *Getting Specific: Postmodern Lesbian Politics*. Whereas Butler's work helps me to describe the way speakers perform multiple identities among determining social discourses, using strategies of subversive repetition to contest the "truths" of heterosexist discourse, Phelan's theory and practice of specificity assists me in addressing and explaining the way speakers create ethos or character to move audiences to action. According to Phelan, "getting specific" means paying attention to "differences [between oneself and one's audience] as important and enduring and difficult and work[ing] not to erase or eliminate those differences" (4). Phelan speaks to the importance of acknowledging differences in identity between ourselves and those we would persuade or work with, emphasizing that acknowledging differences in identity is a starting point for a politics based in issues and coalition rather than on identity and identity politics. The ethic that undergirds a politics of specificity, as Phelan sees it, is grounded in a sustained and serious effort to understand one's own identity-based values and the identity-based values of others. This kind of an ethic, Phelan says, is a starting point for "choice and a conscious fashioning of the self" (157). According to Phelan, a character or ethos based in getting specific about our own and others' identity-based values can enable us to make allies across differences and work to create strategies together that transform oppressive customs, norms, and laws.

Phelan describes these very differences in identity, and thus identity-based values, as multiple and in process rather than as static and monolithic. Seeing oneself and others in terms of static labels and beliefs can lead to either seeing differences as impossible obstacles or to ignoring differences altogether; either strategy leaves in place the customs, norms, and laws that stigmatize those identified as "gay." When instead speakers claim and name their own multiple, in-flux identities, they are more likely to see all people, including those who identify as heterosexual, as complicated and in process rather than as a static enemy image. Likewise, when speakers acknowledge their own multiple and in-process identities, audience members are more likely to see "gay people" as in-process and complicated rather than as a static pariah image.

Getting specific creates a potential space for speakers to look at differences in identity between themselves and others in a new way: as a source of new perspectives and new strategies to address the issue of heterosexism as it interanimates laws, customs, and norms. As speakers do so, they are more able to speak to those who they imagine are "real" allies and also focus on how they might use ethos or character to "make" allies around issues related to heterosexism with those who do not share most or any of their identities or identity-based values. This takes a great deal of patience, willingness, and humility as conflicts inevitably arise when we make room to acknowledge differences as important and real.

In order for students to understand an audience and effectively make allies across differences, we as writing teachers need to foster humility as well as confidence. Students need to be able to recognize how their own specific histories and positions, as well as the discourses around them, constrain their understanding of issues and those who do not share their identity-based values. Students need guidance to work toward honoring and naming their own values and those values their audience holds. Fostering this sort of awareness of the self and others offers students an alternative to reducing issues to black-and-white debates or advocating quick or easy solutions that can be employed only through exercising power over others. As Phelan notes, "getting specific" and inviting others to become allies is slow and often painstaking work; getting specific calls on us to work steadily toward understanding our own values and the values of others as we look for mutually satisfying strategies to address issues.

Both Butler's and Phelan's theories rest on the premise that each person simultaneously inhabits multiple social identities. Though we may, as the student speakers do, foreground one or another identity, we cannot help but read the world from multiple perspectives. As David Wallace notes in his article "Out in the Academy: Heterosexism, Invisibility, and Double Consciousness," "We never speak, listen, read, or write from only one aspect of our identities. In queer inquiry this interrelationship of identity features has been termed intersectionality" (64). The notion of intersectionality is central to the new definition of ethos I am proposing. If we are able to recognize, through self-reflection, how our differing identities are shaping the way we see others and perform our "selves," we are more likely to make conscious choices about how and for whom and for what purpose we are performing our ethos.

This focus on identity points to another central concern in composition: Can we teach writing from an identity perspective so that it leads to rhetorical development instead of "confessional" writing? Will Banks contends that identity-based or embodied writing can "use the 'personal' to make sense of the world, as well as the other way around" (23). According to Banks, embodied writing is related to creative nonfiction—memoir, autobiography, biography, storytelling, and what Victor Villanueva calls "critical autobiography." Embodied writing requires that we acknowledge "the markers of identity . . . (gendered and sexualized)" and attend to "the embodied experiences of our lives" (22). Banks's performance of embodied writing reads a good deal like the stories student speakers tell: Banks performs specific and multiple identities through texts based on his own lived experiences in order to, in his words, make sense of the world and himself. He does not merely "confess" his experiences; he frames them to create meaning for himself and his audience. Banks shows that "good" personal narrative requires a lot of self-knowledge and, I would argue, knowledge of identity as performed among competing social discourses. I see the Bureau cultivating embodied speaking/writing in the student speakers, and what they do is persuasive because it is grounded in specific identity performances. What student speakers do when they tell their stories is "foreground their sense of self at the same time that they consider the social implications of this gesture" (Banks 35). The result of embodied speaking/writing, what I would call specific identity performances, is to call forth reflection in the audience. Banks notes that when he employs embodied writing, it may require reflection and theorizing in others, the same way theirs makes me constantly reevaluate my understanding of the stereotypes I create for their positions. But the price seems so incredibly high I often choose not to pay it. (30)

Banks notes that part of what makes the price of using embodied writing particularly high for him is how he is called to name identities stigmatized in the dominant culture. As a gay man who was raised in a working-class alcoholic home, Banks is acutely aware that writing that draws on these lived experiences is risky and that performing these identities in the classroom is even riskier. As Banks says earlier in his article, "The only thing more dangerous than social class to discuss with students these days is (non-hetero) sex" (25).

It is not difficult to see how student speakers' stories invite the same kind of reevaluation, reflection, and theorizing Banks says embodied writing does or to see the danger or high price involved in such writing/speaking. Student speakers come to the Bureau having already experienced this price and the danger, as we will see more specifically in the next chapter. Nevertheless, student speakers embrace the opportunity to talk to potentially hostile audiences of their peers, to identify publicly as "gay" and tell stories based on their lived experiences, in order to persuade their audiences to work with them against homophobia and heterosexism. This is not easy work; student speakers need communities that are like-minded and understand the danger and the price of such work to sustain themselves and facilitate the kind of rhetorical development that enables them to do this work.

All students need a place or discourse that fosters rhetorical and personal growth, which, as Anne Herrington and Marcia Curtis claim in their book, *Persons in Process: Four Stories of Writing and Personal Development in College,* helps them to "further important personal goals . . . a way of joining with others and linking private with public interests" (35). The desire to connect personal, lived experiences to more public interests is a desire the speakers in this book share with many other students. Herrington and Curtis note that the students in their study "speak of the wish, the tendency to write from personal experience toward something more public, toward essays addressed to an audience capable of understanding and for a kindred group capable of identifying with them" (4–5).

All of the students in Herrington and Curtis's study found discourses or "sponsoring institutions" (34) that enabled them to thrive—to develop as writers and as people. The Bureau was a kind of sponsoring institution for the students in this book; it offered a counter, an outlaw discourse, which assisted them in linking their private needs with their public aims. It is my hope that by investigating the functions of the Bureau, we as teachers of writing may be able to create a classroom that also sponsors students, encouraging each of them to further their own important personal goals, to read the text of their lived experiences as valuable, and to learn, through specific identity performances (embodied speaking/writing), to connect that text to public concerns using academic as well as a variety of other discourses.

Although this book focuses on how students create ethos specifically in relation to heterosexist or homophobic discourses, these are not the only discourses that student speakers contest. The Bureau authorizes student speakers to perform expert and educator identities, contesting what compositionist Linda Brodkey identifies as the role educational discourse defines for students. In her article "On the Subject of Class and Gender in 'The Literacy Letters,'" Brodkey notes that the educational discourse dominant in most schools and universities authorizes teachers to be the experts and educators and to set and authorize topics, which often transcend "class, race, and gender" (656). Correspondingly, students are positioned as the passive recipients of those topics—disallowed to initiate topics, particularly pertaining to class, race, and gender.

The Bureau provides a frame for student speakers to contest this positioning of themselves as students through specific identity performances. It is this frame that I want to explore creating in the writing classroom. In the final chapter of this book, I will address the question of how we as writing teachers might invite students to perform specific identities that are privileged in the academy and to value and assert identities that are not privileged in the academy or larger culture. In this way, I hope we can assist students in our own classrooms to create an ethos that contributes to making allies around issues that are important to them.

In order to do so, students need information about the nature of discourses and how those discourses, beliefs, or "truths" determine their own beliefs. In addition, students need to understand how discourses can interanimate or weave through one another. First, it is important to provide students opportunities to explore the socialization process and identify the values or beliefs they learned in that process.[3] Second, students need examples of how discourses interanimate each other. For example, heterosexist discourse can shape legal discourse; can position those identified as GLBT as criminals by definition and as non-people; can convey the worldview that the only "true" and legal expression of sexuality is that of the heterosexual, married, procreative pair; and can actively constitute knowledge that supports compulsory heterosexuality and denies the existence or legality of non-heterosexual expression and partnerships. The existence of heterosexist discourse shapes how students understand who gay people are and leads to, for example, the use of the phrase, "That's so gay," to mean, "That's stupid."

We can show students how language as various discourses shapes our material circumstances, our reality, by constituting our social relationships, identity, and the power that circulates through the social system. For example, a question that is often asked on Bureau presentations is about the legal status of gay marriage. Speakers typically address this question in two ways: by referencing any stories they have about the lack of legal recognition gay couples face or by mentioning the legislation that exists that forbids the recognition of gay marriage. In the process, speakers are able to show audiences how heterosexist discourse together with legal discourse has made it possible for a number of "Defense of Marriage Acts" (DOMAs)[4] to be passed at the federal and state government levels; these amendments effectively bar men partnered with men and women partnered with women from the rights enjoyed by their legally married heterosexual counterparts. Speakers are able to then point to how they themselves or couples they know have been denied family health insurance and social security survivor benefits, two of the most common material effects of DOMAs. Speakers also tell their audiences about groups of individuals that have asserted their agency and used outlaw discourse to interanimate legal discourse and made it possible for one civil union amendment that recognizes non-heterosexual couples to be passed and ratified in the state of Vermont and for legal gay marriage to be initiated in the state of Massachusetts. Often speakers also reference a number of local and state ordinances that forbid discrimination based on sexual orientation in regard to employment, housing, and public accommodations.

By pointing out the existence of DOMAs, civil unions, and legal gay marriage, student speakers are able to emphasize, by illustration, the major tenet of identity performance theory: we can never be entirely free of or outside of discourse and its determining power, nor are we wholly determined by it. We can and do frequently assert our agency to contest, through outlawed identity performances, the "truth" of various normative social discourses and in turn assert subjugated "truths."

The theory of specificity offers a practical political alternative with its focus on making allies who differ in significant ways from us. For example, Bureau speakers need not insist on inviting only those who identify as "gay" to join them in challenging DOMAs or supporting the legalization of civil unions or gay marriage. Instead, speakers can focus on making allies of those who do not share their identities, noting the very real differences as well as the similarities between people as they work to create strategies to address issues. For example, speakers can invite those who identify in many different ways to work together to assure that all citizens have the right to choose with whom they partner and to have that relationship legally recognized, or to assure that all citizens have the right to protection against discrimination and violence based on sexual orientation.

All students who are able—as the student speakers in this study were—to understand how various discourses are positioning them can choose to create specific rhetorical identity constructions in their writing. We can then show students how they might perform their ethos in ways that address an audience whom they are in turn positioning as potential allies around issues of importance to them. We can remind students that these allies need not share the students' particular social identities to share their understanding of an issue.

In this book, I explore the ways the Speaker's Bureau apparently enabled the student speakers to sort the "truths" embedded in social discourses and to make choices about how specifically to perform GLBT identities. We will see how the Bureau helped student speakers come to critical consciousness about the relationship of the self to the social forces moving through language as discourse that in turn shaped their material reality. In the following chapters, we will see how the students in this book used language in order to contest the "truths" of heterosexist discourse. In Bureau presentations, editorials, and papers for classes, student speakers repositioned themselves from "queer," occupying a stigmatized subject position, to a variety of multiple positions: "not so far from you" (a student, a family member, an athlete). We will also see how student speakers used an outlaw discourse that offered a positive subject position, a "down-to-earth" social identity for those identified as gay, and introduced altogether new definitions of "queer," taking back that word and others like it as terms of pride and strength and militancy.

We will also see how including speakers who identified as allies on the Bureau and encouraging all speakers to claim their multiple and specific social identities created a new discourse of specificity and a new relationship to differences. Not only is "sameness" no longer required in order to work together on issues (Phelan 158), but using this new discourse of specificity also allows speakers on the Bureau to begin the work of disarticulating a hierarchy that stigmatizes some differences while valorizing others. This is an important step in using ethos to invite/make allies who recognize and are willing to address injustice.

In this book, I want to advance our field's understanding of the nature of ethos as a rhetorical strategy by examining the specific identity performances of Vincente and the other speakers as well as the way the Bureau functions as a sponsoring institution for student speakers. In doing so, we can sharpen our understanding of ethos in all rhetorical work, including our understanding of how we might use identity performance and specificity in our own writing classrooms. In the next section, I describe my own role as the author of this study, detailing the specific identity performances I too perform and have performed.

## Performing (My)Self(s)

Identity construction is an essential focus for composition. As David Wallace points out, focusing on the performative nature of identity can enable writers to become aware of the social discourses that shape their identities and to make conscious choices about whether to participate in or resist and transform heterosexism, racism, sexism, and other forms of oppressions (53). The concept of embodied writing is important to specific identity performance. As Jane Hindman asserts, embodied writing "require[s] me to surrender my analytic need to be right and/or absolute in my understanding of how language [and life] works" as well as creates an "unflinching self-reflection, maintaining a relentless awareness of the ways I use rhetoric to position myself" (101). Embodied writing echoes what Phelan calls for, humility and awareness of our multiple performances of identities and how we are using rhetoric to persuade our audiences to become allies. Like Banks and Hindman and others who advocate including the personal in academic professional writing, I too am choosing to weave theory with my own embodied writing, my own performance of my own specific multiple identities. I choose to do so as an example of what I will be doing throughout this text—showing how the student speakers performed multiple identities in multiple contexts—and of how we might use these examples to inform our classroom practice of teaching writing.

> My name is Zan Gonçalves; I work here at the college. I teach college writing, literature, and writing for social action as well as performance studies. I've lived in this area since 1993 but grew up in California.

By the time I was in sixth grade, I was aware that, like my best friends who were boys, I too was smitten with girls. My best friend Tom Sharp and I were class clowns and competed with each other for the attention of the lovely Mary Ramirez. I got a C in citizenship that year. By seventh grade, my classmates had branded me a "girl who didn't like any boys." My friendships with boys didn't count, while my obvious romantic interest in girls made me an outcast. My family moved the following year, and I started over in a new school, intent this time on hiding my attraction to girls.

It was also during elementary and middle school that I first realized that race/ethnicity and social class matter. I learned that my family's Portuguese and Mexican ways of being as well as our physical characteristics were considered "not quite white" by some and not Portuguese or Mexican enough by others; I learned that the working-class values my parents brought into their new middle-class lives were "not quite right" according to some and fine according to others. I didn't feel like a fit-in anywhere.

I noticed how there were only two people identified by others as gay in the rural northern California town where I grew up: Cindy, a white girl in high school who was tall, muscular, and painfully shy; and Tommy, a white middle-aged man who lisped and pranced and lived with his mother in town. More than once I heard my classmates call Cindy a "dyke" or read, "Cindy's a dyke," written on a chalkboard. As for Tommy, rumor had it that he had sex with men for six-packs of Coca-Cola. The thought of being identified with these two people terrified me. I slid through both my high school and my undergraduate years in a fog—smoking lots of pot and drinking lots of beer and falling in love with my best girl friends.

I never told anyone how I felt until I was twenty-three. I got tired of living in what felt like a lie, a pressure cooker, and I came bursting out of the closet. That year, 1985, I joined my first speaker's bureau at California State University, Chico, and began the work I still do: educating people about the effects of homophobia and heterosexism in all our lives, inviting people to work with me against discrimination based on sexual preference in particular, and helping people see how all discrimination is linked, how none of us can be full citizens in a real democracy until discrimination based on gender, race, class, ability, and sexual preference is eliminated.

This "story" takes about three minutes to tell. In that short time I perform a variety of identities. Like the other speakers, I begin by constructing and performing myself as an insider, a teacher at the college. I follow with stories of best friends, crushes, and misbehaving as a young adolescent and of using pot and beer to dull the pain of not fitting in as a young adult. All these performances position me as an insider or at least a recognizable outsider, inviting my audience to recall their own experiences at those ages. I weave a performance of myself as a stigmatized outsider through these insider performances: my romantic interest in other girls, my outcast status, and my experience of being in between ethnic and class categories. I also reference Cindy and Tommy and how others positioned them as stigmatized outsiders and my own fear of becoming an outsider alone. I end my story by positioning myself again as an insider, an educator working for social justice.

Looking back, I can see that by the time I was thirteen, I knew intuitively my lived experiences around gender and sexuality fell outside the possible, intelligible subject positions, the "truths" offered by dominant discourses of sexism and heterosexism. I understood viscerally how transgressing normative gender roles, in particular expressing same-sex attraction, leads one to be positioned by heterosexist/sexist discourses as incoherent and literally unbelievable. As a speaker and observer, I have heard many an audience member say during the question/answer period of a panel presentation, "I just don't *believe in* homosexuality or gay people." Judith Butler notes that those who do not conform to dominant gender role norms simply aren't regarded as persons if they are unintelligible in the gender system (17). This is what the students in this book and I are resisting, being positioned as non-people because of our expression of same-sex attraction as well as other non-normative expressions of gender identity.

This gender system is undergirded by what Adrienne Rich defines as compulsory heterosexuality—a component of heterosexist discourse that literally demands only heterosexual expressions. Butler states that it is compulsory heterosexuality that makes "true" a causal relationship between sex, gender, and desire as in "penis=man= heterosexuality" (25). Just as I did, the students in this book and those in our classrooms discover as children how to perform the "right" gender, to be "good" girls and boys for the all-important audience of our families and later our peers in order to get our needs for safety and belonging at least minimally met.

Butler maintains that all gender is at base performative, and we perform our genders largely through language. This idea that we perform and construct our social identities and in turn are shaped by ideologies such as the gender system is counter to the Cartesian notion that identity is essential, fixed, and unitary. Instead, identity performance theory posits that identity is performed and constructed, in-flux and multiple, created for particular local contexts to be created anew for still other contexts. This holds for all social identities, including race and social class.

Like the students in this book, I realize now it was on the first speaker's bureau I joined that I began to understand experientially just how "fluid and multiple" identity and the "truth" could be. The members of this speaker's bureau were from a variety of backgrounds, but they were all committed to educating others about what they called the "myths and facts about homosexuality." They disrupted the compulsory heterosexual gender system in ways I had at that time never conceived of. For example, at one end of the spectrum was Cassandra, whose body was identifiable as African American and male. Cassandra lived as a woman and was attracted to men who were also male-bodied but instead lived as men and were also attracted to men. My mind spun—why didn't her lovers date "real" women instead of a man in a dress? If Cassandra enjoyed being a woman, why didn't she have surgery to become one? What was incoherent for me in the beginning became coherent as I learned about these people and their stories. In this way, I encountered a new discourse that made visible and believable the ways in which all of us construct and perform a variety of multiple identities. I began to realize that what was "true" and possible in one discourse was not in another. Heterosexist discourse made Cassandra and her lovers non-people, unintelligible. The outlaw discourse I began to learn with Cassandra made her and her lovers real, coherent, and valuable people. Similarly, when the students in this book told their stories on Bureau presentations, they offered their audience a new discourse and a sense of the ways in which identity is specific, multiple, fluid, constructed, and finally performed.

The speaker's bureau I joined in 1985, like the one in this book, acted as a sponsoring institution for me. It provided me with a forum where I could position myself as an educator and expert; with a new lens that allowed me to see other non-normative, outlaw "truths" and re-see and value my own lived experiences; and with strategies to re-story myself for an audience I wished to make into allies. Coming out of the closet—publicly claiming and affirming my homosexuality—enabled me to find what I have come to think of as an outlaw life, a life larger than compulsory heterosexuality and gender hierarchy.

The first speaker's bureau I joined offered me an alternative to power-relations in the dominant culture; and, though I couldn't identify it then, it created a space for me to position myself in a new way, giving me a community and an outlaw discourse I shared with this community, new words and new definitions for words I already knew. In northern California, "the Castro" referred not just to a district in San Francisco but to the "gay" district, and hence a reference to visiting the Castro was a coded way to reveal one's homosexuality. The words "family" and "church" acquired new meanings—asking another gay friend if so-and-so was "a member of the family/church" was a coded way of asking if that person was gay. I learned the word "heterosexism" and learned to "read" jokes about the supposedly dangerous, disgusting, out-of-control sexuality of the homosexual in a new way—as "heterosexist"—rather than to "read" these jokes as I always had, as the God-given truth of homosexuality as a crime, a sin, a sickness. I learned from the "Myths and Facts about Homosexuality" sheet the speaker's bureau provided that homosexuality had been taken off the list of psychiatric disorders in the early 1970s and that there had been organizations in the United States devoted to the civil rights of people who identified as gay and lesbian since the 1930s.

I was, without realizing it, acquiring a new outlaw discourse and worldview; graduate school became the place where I began to examine the social and political forces I had experienced growing up, looking particularly at the way language could be used to reproduce or transform these social and political forces. I continued to speak on Bureau presentations and as such was very much an insider.

As Beverly Moss notes in her article "Ethnography and Composition: Studying Language at Home," there are advantages to being an insider, to studying one's own community. Often insiders are able to "discern patterns and attach meaning more quickly and with less difficulty" than outsiders can (163). However, insiders are just as likely to overlook patterns because of their familiarity with the community. Such was my case. The Speaker's Bureau panel presentations were, after more than ten years as a speaker, so familiar to me that I could not really "see" that panel presentations provided speakers with a unique forum. It was a colleague who helped me realize that panel presentations did provide speakers with a particular forum that positioned them as experts and educators, insiders to the dominant culture.[5] Later, as I coded these same panel presentations, I realized "expert and educator" were not the only social identities in which speakers positioned themselves. As I noted above, students positioned and constructed themselves alternately as insiders and outsiders in a variety of social identities. This became particularly important as I began to explore the relationship of each speaker's ethos to audience.

## Sponsoring Institutions and the Performance of Identities

Chapter 2 explores how to best facilitate the rhetorical growth of students by examining the ways student speakers learned to do the work they did and what they gained from the Bureau as a sponsoring institution. We will also see how student speakers used specificity and identity performance for Bureau panel presentations through the stories they told and the dialogues they facilitated with their audiences.

Chapter 3 examines how we might facilitate crossover effect and better ensure that rhetorical development in one context might lead to writing success in another context. In case studies of two of these student speakers, we can see how a conscious focus on specific identity performance led them to use a range of identity performances to negotiate a variety of discourses, from private journals to academic essays to letters to the editor. We'll see how a conscious understanding of specific identity performance helped these student speakers to make transfers across contexts.

The final two chapters detail how we might teach writing based on identity so that it leads to rhetorical development and not "confessional" writing by introducing our students to the principles of specific identity performance. In the process, we will explore the writing classroom as a potential site for the kind of sponsorship the Bureau provides. I will introduce a range of strategies that invite students to write from new subject positions, for example, as fellow writers and thinkers engaged in dialogue with published authors of academic essays; as researchers engaged in conducting small surveys of their peers and analyzing and interpreting their data in light of a particular purpose and audience; and as citizens, invested in creating changes in their communities through the use of an open letter. Chapter 5 offers us an opportunity to think about how each of us might better assist all our students in using language to negotiate academic as well as other discourses and in the process claim a positive sense of self, capable of using language to thrive in the academy and to contribute to their own communities.

# 2 / Exploring What It Means to Speak a New Ideology

We're here and real people. We live everywhere.

—Peggy James

If we believe, as many do, that paying attention to identity issues and social forces facilitates rhetorical growth for all our students, then how exactly do we incorporate these elements into our writing classrooms? Those who have grappled with this question—Anne Herrington and Marcia Curtis, Elizabeth Chiseri-Strater, and Linda Brodkey, to name a few—have noted how the teaching of traditional school writing has virtually ignored issues of identity and social discourses, components that I believe are central in developing rhetorical savvy.

By rhetorical savvy, I mean the sort of attention to ethos I noted in Vincente's story and the way he described what he was doing as a rhetor on Speaker's Bureau panels. As I explained in the previous chapter, Vincente was not an anomaly; all of the student speakers and speakers-to-be I met had some degree of what I am calling rhetorical savvy. Peggy James was no different. I met Peggy, a brand-new member of the Bureau, at one of the several training workshops I attended for people who wished to become speakers on the Bureau. She used the words quoted above to wrap up her "story," the one she was practicing to tell on Bureau panel presentations. Peggy hoped her story would begin to convince her peers that homophobia and heterosexism are unnecessary. This was what she wanted her audience, her peers, to remember: that she and others who identify as gay are indeed "real" and "people," living "everywhere" or at least in most towns and cities in the United States. I could tell by the way Peggy said it that she was trying on this outlaw "truth"; it was new for her to assert publicly what she knew privately from her own lived experience. She and the others at the training were well aware of the homophobic ideology, the dominant "truth" about "gay" people as "unreal" and "subhuman" or simply as "bad" humans inhabiting the unseemly margins of society.

The Bureau's training workshops created a space for Peggy and the other speakers on the Bureau to examine their identities and to question the dominant ideology of homophobia and heterosexism and to use their lived experiences to forge new outlaw ideologies, connecting the personal with the public. The Bureau guided these student speakers to represent themselves as people, as subjects and agents of social change, and to offer this new ideology to their peers. In the process, these student speakers grew as rhetors.

In the previous chapter, I discussed Linda Brodkey's take on educational discourse, how it positions students as passive recipients and restricts discourse on class, race, and gender—topics central to examining the role of identity and social discourses in shaping student writing and encouraging rhetorical growth. When Brodkey tells us that "catsup is to vegetables as school writing is to writing" in her autoethnography "Writing on the Bias" (31), she is addressing a prevailing concern in the profession: how can students grow rhetorically if school writing is "taught solely as knowing and following the rules" (29)? Instead, Brodkey would have us "see writing as an invitation to identify, analyze, and critique anything and everything that represents itself as unarguably true" (23). Clearly, "rules" of writing qualify as subjects for analysis and critique as do other "truths" embedded in differing discourses. In Brodkey's article "Articulating Poststructural Theory in Research on Literacy," she discusses the importance of paying attention to social discourses. As I explained above, Brodkey is particularly concerned with how educational discourses disallow certain topics in the classroom and position students as passive receivers of information and rules. She states the necessity of questioning the "truths" of educational discourse, noting, "It is the authority of the state in the person of the teacher that makes educational discourse consequential" ("Articulating" 23). Brodkey proposes critical literacy as a practice aimed at demystifying educational and other discourses, "an approach to teaching that insists on the students' right to learn how to conduct themselves as writers of the world" able to "lay out a case in support of a position in a variety of genres" (23). Providing students with a place, a pedagogy, where they can speak new ideologies into existence is one way to encourage students to grow as rhetors and people.

Chiseri-Strater is also concerned with how students negotiate educational discourses and structures in higher education and grow rhetorically. In her book *Academic Literacies: The Public and Private Discourse of University Students,* she follows two students through their college careers, noting how they experienced their education as fragmented. Both students found literacies that helped them organize their experiences, discourses grounded in their particular identities. For example, Nick, who majored in political science, used a journal where he created his own political cartoons to make sense of and to write his own take on the world and his place in it. Chiseri-Strater makes a case for paying attention to identity and social discourses as we mentor students.

Anne Herrington and Marcia Curtis contend that all students need this sort of mentoring or space to begin to see themselves as agents able to make sense of the world and to address publicly what is most important to them privately. Like Chiseri-Strater's students, the students in Herrington and Curtis's book, *Persons in Process,* were seeking a way to make sense of their educational experiences. As their longitudinal study proceeded, Herrington and Curtis saw how students found discourses that assisted them in beginning to make sense of the multiple and conflicting discourses they were encountering, inside and outside the classroom.

If we believe that students need a space in which to examine the social discourses they experience via their identities in order to grow as rhetors, then it is important to consider how we as writing teachers might create that space in our classrooms. Like the Bureau training workshops, we can ground our pedagogy in specific identity performance, creating a type of critical pedagogy and sponsorship in the writing classroom. As I will demonstrate further in the last two chapters, we can use this pedagogy to invite students to participate in exercises designed to assist them in seeing how they consciously construct themselves rhetorically. For example, at the beginning of the required first-year writing workshops I teach, I ask students to draw a picture symbolizing how they feel about writing and write three words that describe them as writers. Typically, when we share these representations with one another, a few students seem to resist being positioned as a writer altogether and offer pictures of themselves snoring in bed with words like "boring"; most seem to position themselves as struggling writers and draw pictures of climbing steep mountains with words like "slow"; and a very few seem to take up the position of writer and draw pictures of flowers and trees with words like "creative."

After we've listened to one another's representations, I ask students what they've noticed, and as I list the words for them on the blackboard, I call attention to how it is we are using language to represent ourselves to one another. This exercise is meant to invite students into the social identity of "writer," an identity that holds a valued position in educational discourse. I see this as an important part of assisting students in becoming agents, in countering an educational discourse that provides unsatisfying subject positions for those identified as "students," passive recipients of knowledge. Again, if we believe that students' rhetorical growth is linked to an awareness of identity and social discourses, then we will want to find ways to introduce these concepts in our classrooms. In order to consider how we might do so, the remainder of this chapter explores how the Speaker's Bureau implicitly uses the theory of specific identity performance to create a sponsoring institution where student speakers have the opportunity to examine their identities in relation to social discourses and learn how to use ethos to link their private needs for respect and safety as "gay" people to their public aim of social justice as speakers on the Bureau.

In the first part of this chapter, I will examine the way the Speaker's Bureau operates as a sponsoring institution—its structure, content, effect, and the individual development that goes on within Bureau programs. I will explore the ways Bureau training invited the students in this book into the valued social identities of "expert" and "educator," offering them more satisfying subject positions from which to perform their identities. I will also look at how the training guided students to value and use their lived experiences, teaching them to select and story these experiences and then revise their stories in order to move particular audiences.

The second part of the chapter focuses on what the student speakers did with the training. Using transcripts from Bureau panel discussions, I will show how speakers performed their identities among competing social discourses, creating a complex ethos that redefines "gay people." I will also show how Butler's idea of strategies of subversive repetition functions as speakers redefined words and jokes used to stigmatize "gay people." In addition, I will also demonstrate how all the speakers strove to create allies by illuminating the link between words used to oppress "gay people" and the material consequences of those words.

## Positioning the Self as Expert

Bureau training workshops are central in how students learn to construct themselves rhetorically, how they position themselves and perform insider and outsider identities, and how they educate their peers. The Speaker's Bureau training workshops facilitate rhetorical growth in part by emphasizing the importance of valuing one's lived experiences or "stories" and, of course, the sexual identities of the students. When Peggy James says, "We're here and real people. We live everywhere," she constructs herself as "real" and central rather than unreal and marginal.

Similarly, when Moe Pontiack—one of the five focal students in this book—then a twenty-year-old junior who introduced herself to her peers as someone who was Jewish, lesbian, and a social activist, told me in an interview, "To just say, like, 'I'm human and this is my story,' it seems to do a lot," she was creating a rhetorical construction of herself as "human" and reflecting on the idea that stories can and do move audiences. Below is an excerpt of how Moe performed specific identities, creating an ethos of "lesbian as human" for her college-aged peers:

> I'm Moe, I'm twenty, a junior. I grew up with a happy childhood, twin sister, and two loving parents. I had a vague

sense of conflict, friction regarding the ways my parents
wanted me to dress and act. . . .

About sixth or seventh grade, my classmates decided I
was a lesbian. Funny, 'cause I hadn't yet. I got beaten and ha-
rassed; I was scared for my life. I wanted to live, but it seemed
like it was my fault, that I was doing something horrible.

Moe noted that to construct herself in this way "seems to do a
lot" toward changing "the average person's mind about homophobia." It is this conscious link student speakers learned to make between how they constructed and performed their identities rhetorically and their aims as writers and speakers that I wish to make explicit,
to teach to the students in all my classes. Moe seemed to have learned
to grasp the importance of this link among ethos, audience, and purpose in part because the job of positioning oneself as "real" and "human" for those identified as GLBT is ongoing in a culture where heterosexist discourse is pervasive. In part, it is the training that speakers
receive from the Bureau training workshops that emphasize the importance of being conscious of this link.

The Bureau also emphasizes the importance of positioning oneself. As I said, the Bureau is a unique forum that positions students
as active agents: speakers, educators, and experts authorized to discuss sexual identity as well as related identity issues and civil rights.
Speakers internalize this positioning and position themselves in these
ways. In her interview with me, Moe told me that she continued to
speak for the Speaker's Bureau because she believed that positioning herself as "human" and telling her story was "the most effective
way to educate people about gay and lesbian issues." Her comment
clearly shows that she had taken up the social identity of educator.

This is the forum students invoke when they enter a dorm or
classroom to speak; it is an unusual position for students in the academy. As I noted above, educational discourse positions students as
passive recipients, not as those who set and authorize topics. In addition, the topics these students forward and discuss are often dis-
qualified in the classroom, along with other topics seen to have a
political charge. The Bureau teaches students to name and claim their
own specific set of identities and to value and use those identities in

order to make a conscious link between the identities they perform and the strategies they use to connect with and move an audience. Speakers tell stories that highlight both similarities and differences between themselves and their audiences as a strategy. It is in this complex performance of multiple identities that students learn to position themselves as educators on the topic of homophobia, shifting to a valued insider's subject position in educational discourse and introducing an outlaw discourse as well as discourse around political action in order to persuade their audiences to resist and challenge homophobia.

The exercises students learn at workshops assist them in constructing embodied stories, storying their lived experiences and performing identities for particular audiences in their opening stories and in their dialogues with a variety of audiences. The students in this book, like many of the students in our classrooms, had private needs and public aims and wished to connect the two. In this case, the student speakers' most apparent need was to create positive rhetorical constructions of themselves as GLBT, and their most apparent aim was to create a safe space at the university to inhabit those social identities. The students began, through the Bureau's assistance, by seeing themselves as educators and experts. They continued to position themselves as insiders to a variety of discourses dominant in the academy as they learned in Bureau workshops to tell stories constructed from the texts of their lived experiences. Students performed many specific social identities that were recognizable as insiders relative to these discourses: as students, family members, sorority members, basketball players, music fans, and so on. In doing so, they invited their audiences to identify with them.

The students also re-valenced what it means to claim and perform a GLBT identity—storying their lived experiences and showing how the discourse of heterosexism positioned them as outsiders in the dominant culture. In the process, speakers were able to articulate how heterosexist discourse wove through the discourses of law, religion, and the codes for mental and physical health. The outlaw discourse that students introduced and connected to the above discourses served to position them again as insiders. In essence, they began the work of teaching this alternative, subjugated outlaw discourse to their peers—offering their peers alternate "truths," new ways of understanding what it might mean to be gay. In the process, students transmuted formerly outsider positions—those stigmatized by a variety of discourses—to insider positions that were both valued and valorized.

Like the opening exercise I use in my first-year writing courses, Bureau training workshops begin by offering alternate subject positions to students and inviting them, in this case, to specifically link their "gay" identity to the other social identities they perform. The opening exercise of the workshops I attended asked students the following:

- Introduce yourself and tell us a little of your personal history.
- Tell us what you like about your sexual orientation.
- What is your biggest fear about speaking?
- Tell us why you want to become a speaker on the Bureau.

These prompts led students to begin reflecting on their lived experiences and invited them to re-valence their subject positions relative to their sexual identity, to speak about what they "liked" about this contentious position. This is how students began to shift positions, to think of themselves as speakers and educators who draw on the texts of their lived experiences.

Before students began to construct their stories, they worked together with Katie O'Connor, the graduate student who facilitated the two training workshops I attended, to define what it means to educate people, to perform the social identity of educator. Students brainstormed about this identity they were considering taking up, defining in particular the difference between an activist and an educator. Together they defined activists as outsiders in the dominant educational discourse. They noted that activists are positioned as valued insiders in many gay civil rights organizations and in outlaw discourse and various political discourses. Indeed, the Speaker's Bureau program explicitly values the work of those who get the issues out into the public domain through demonstrations and other means. Workshop members agreed that educators also introduce issues into the public arena and that the subject position educators occupy is a respected one at the university, clearly an insider position in educational discourse. According to Katie, an educator is able to "sit back and listen to things that are difficult . . . and ask herself, 'How am I going to try to educate people, not scare people by being too weird or too angry?'" Implicit in this question is the recognition of what is valued and what is not in the dominant discourse of the academy. A degree of conformity and a restrained expression of emotion are valued in educational discourse. Most students on the Bureau reflected these values to their audiences, carefully cultivating shared values like these and focusing on how GLBT folks are simply "not so far from you." This was an ethos-building move that enabled students to shift positions from "too weird or too angry," characteristics projected on to activists, to educators who listened carefully and responded kindly in order to build bridges of understanding between themselves and their audiences.

In Bureau training workshops, students began constructing their rhetorical selves by drawing life-maps. Using large sheets of newsprint and colored pens, they mapped the highlights of their life experiences, particularly those events or moments when they recognized or claimed their present sexual identities. Students told one another these stories using the life-map as a prop and then began to discuss how to select particular vignettes from the life-map in order to construct a five- to ten-minute opening story for Bureau panel presentations to classes and dorms. The facilitator led students to identify those pieces of their lived experiences that their audience members might recognize and identify with and to open their stories with those vignettes. As students constructed their opening stories, selecting and revising vignettes that showed what it has been like for them to recognize and claim their present sexual identity, the facilitator reminded them to incorporate the following:

- Speak for yourself (use I-statements) to disable assumptions that all gay people are alike and thus address stereotyping of all gay people.
- Use vignettes that might evoke the sort of questions from the audience you want to introduce and address.

- Choose vignettes that set a particular tone, and consider how to invite humor, if possible, as a way to bring ease to a traditionally loaded topic.
- Select stories that convey what you enjoy about being who you are to counter the pervasive belief that "gay" people are unhappy with their "gayness."
- Tell vignettes that connect with particular audiences (attend to age, ethnicity, and the like, and use vignettes that focus on what it was like to be that age or on how your own ethnicity/race intersects with your sexual identity).

To close the story, student speakers invited questions, a dialogue with the audience members, having introduced ground rules before they began telling their stories. These ground rules emphasized confidentiality for speakers and audience members; asserted that "there are no stupid questions"; stipulated that speakers reserved the right to refuse to answer a question deemed too personal; and invited audience members to add their own ground rules in an attempt to create a space where all who were present had their needs for safety and respect met as much as possible. It was the student speakers who set the ground rules and who set and policed the agenda—opening with stories, inviting dialogue with the audience members, and closing by offering suggestions to the audience on how individual audience members might address homophobia. This structure allowed student speakers to connect important personal needs to public aims.

The choices student speakers made were based on the time frame they had, the purpose, the subject matter, and a particular audience. Once the ground rules were established, student speakers used vignettes chosen from their lived experiences for an explicit purpose, in this case to invite "audience members to grapple with issues of oppression . . . [and] offer a human voice and face to people whom society continues to construct as 'other'" (*Speaker's Bureau Manual* 2). All student speakers consciously used their opening stories to change their audience's beliefs about those identified as GLBT and did so by presenting, as Moe noted, "gay people as human . . . and complicated." The process of creating an opening story led student speakers to value their lived experiences as texts they could use to accomplish their public aims. What follows are examples of how student speakers performed identities and introduced new "truths" in their opening stories.

## Performing a Specific Self

Student speakers use the rhetorical training they receive from the Bureau to tell vignettes in which they perform specific insider and outsider identities, performing their "selves" to non-ally and poten-tial-ally groups on the university campus in order to

- invite their audiences to identify with them by creating an ethos based in specificity;
- show how heterosexist discourse positions them as "other";
- explain the strategies they used to cope (here we'll recog-nize Butler's ideas of the performance of identity and strat-egies of subversive repetition as survival strategies in re-sponse to conflicting social discourses);
- describe how they finally found an alternative community, a sponsoring institution;
- and again invite the audience members to identify with them and become allies.

Students use the vignettes to perform a variety of social identities, as insiders and outsiders relative to dominant discourses and the dominant "truths" these discourses define—particularly heterosex-ist and educational discourses. Student speakers also use subjugated discourses—specifically outlaw discourse—to reposition themselves as insiders to subjugated cultures and to valorize subject positions vilified in the dominant culture. Below are two opening stories from two different panel presentations, one from Viany and one from Sulli.

### Viany Rivera's Story

Hi, I'm Viany, I'm a sophomore and an architecture major. I live in Southwest [name of dorm], and I'm an RA up there. And I'm actually in a sorority.

I came out when I was a freshman in high school a little over five years ago. When I told my mother, she cried, and she still cries; she still hopes I'll get married. That's okay.

When I was a sophomore in high school, I tried to kill myself, and the same thing happened like a year later after that. Sophomore and junior year. It was funny that I was actually class historian for like three years. All my closest friends came out too. So all my girl friends and guy friends were all gay, and that was weird. It was okay. And we got a program in my high school that helped me out, helped us out. I didn't want to kill myself anymore. That was a Safe Schools program.

I came to college and met a lot of different people, which really, really helped. I think I picked UMass . . . not just [because of] the music program but because there's so much diversity on campus. I could be in a sorority and be gay and do everything I want. That's it.

These stories are not easy to hear or tell. Though Viany began and ended on a positive note, emphasizing the insider social identities she performed as student, sorority member, and RA, the vignette also tells and shows how heterosexist discourse positions Viany as "other," as an outsider in stigmatized subject positions because she identified and was identified as lesbian. Her story followed the pattern she learned in the training workshops: begin with an insider performance, reference the effect of being positioned as an outsider, and end with a reference to finding a community where it is relatively safe to inhabit what the dominant culture sees as conflicting roles ("be in a sorority and be gay"). Notably, Viany did not choose to reference her ethnicity—Puerto Rican—in her opening story, which would mark her as an outsider in the dominant culture; nor did she position herself as an insider to the Puerto Rican community. In her interview with me, she spoke of how other Puerto Rican high school students shunned her when she came out, telling her she should "act Puerto Rican," not "white." Clearly, these students had in mind just how to correctly perform a Puerto Rican identity, and claiming a lesbian identity was not part of that picture.

Sulli began as Viany did, referencing his student status and his status as a family member as well as his ethnicity that simultaneously marked him as an insider to the dominant culture and somehow outside it as well when he explained that his family was a "very traditional European family." Sulli was first-generation Austrian American and Catholic and was very aware of his father's family and their ethnic traditions and history. At one point in his opening story, Sulli told the audience that his father was one of three survivors of an extended family of thirty-seven, the rest of whom were killed during World War II.

### Excerpts from Sulli Schwartz's Story

My name is Sulli. I'm a history and anthro major. . . . I come from a traditional European family, old money. . . .

One of my first memories, I think, was at my friend Eric's house. We were watching this movie, *Stand by Me*. . . . I didn't realize till later that I had a crush on them [the boys in the movie]. I spent all my time with Mark [a friend he met in England one summer]. . . . We experimented a little. We didn't think anything of it. . . . I never told anyone.

Third semester of my freshman year [in high school], I had been checking out this guy Paul all over the place. It was then that it clicked into my head, that I made the connection with being gay. . . . The town [where he grew up] was very anti-Semitic, very homophobic. So, I instantly became very stressed out about this, and I kept it to myself for a very long time. . . . So, a year later I basically had a nervous fit and ran down to my social worker and told him. I came out to a few friends, my Roman Catholic priest. . . . At that point the priest said, "I can't help you with this one." He said, "It might be in your best interest to find another place to pray." Which I did.

I was so afraid of being outed. . . . I had such a feeling of fear and isolation driven into me that I just accepted my decision [to refuse to help Adrienne, a female friend who requested help from him regarding a boyfriend who was abusive]. It was a month and half later that the other friend told me Adrienne had been date raped [by the abusive boyfriend]. I decided I would come out to everyone [after months of self-blame and self-imposed isolation]. I felt if I came out to everyone, there was no chance that my homosexuality, my gayness, would cause harm to anyone else again.

I came out to my mother. . . . I tried to tell her, "I don't know if you should tell Dad." Since I acted effeminately, he [his father] thought it was aristocratic, when it was actually being gay. It got tenser and tenser at home, and at school I was getting beaten up. I then moved to New York City with my sister, and life went on. I saw myself separating myself from the straight community more and more. . . . I then came to UMass after finally finishing up high school and starting to mend my relationship with my parents.

As I noted in chapter 1, Sulli and the other speakers' opening stories were a complex performance of insider and outsider identities that destabilized the idea of a static and unitary "gay" identity. The frame of the Speaker's Bureau presentations gave student speakers a way to use the text of their lived experiences to reposition themselves from passive recipients of alienation and violence to active agents able to address and challenge the oppression perpetuated by heterosexist and other stereotyping discourses. Sulli's story highlighted how his awareness of heterosexist discourse shaped his experience: in his omissions, what he did not tell; in the reactions of others—the priest, his parents, students at school; and his own performance of a "passing," "straight" self. Like Viany, Sulli ended his vignette with the story of finding a like-minded community, a kind of sponsoring institution, people who apparently assisted Sulli in seeing himself as someone able to "mend" the relationship between himself and his parents.

All student speakers chose to position themselves in a variety of social identities that were identifiable as insider subject positions to the discourses that defined dominant culture. Like Sulli, Vincente also referenced insider/outsider subject positions around his ethnicity. In his opening story, Vincente noted, "I come from a strong Hispanic community, so I would've never come out in high school." He also reported a humorous conversation between himself and his mother in his opening story—first in Spanish and then in English for the audience, clearly signaling his insider status in this community.

Jamar Evans did this as well, weaving in references to his insider subject position in the African American community when he says, "I grew up in the South Bronx . . . which is predominantly, where I grew up, black and Spanish," and ends his story emphasizing, "I was black . . . I was always proud of myself." Jamar—at the time a twenty-one-year-old senior who identified as African American, gay, and a psychology major—included in his story his social identity as a member of the GLBT community, an outsider, and followed it with much about his insider status as a member of a loving family, a basketball player, and so on. Jamar also asserted his insider membership as a black man, though that positioned him outside the dominant culture:

### Jamar Evans's Story

My name is Jamar and I'm a senior here studying psychology, hopefully to go into social or clinical psych of the gay and lesbian movement. I grew up in the South Bronx of New York City . . . which is predominantly, where I grew up, black and Spanish. I grew up in a loving household—two older sisters, one older brother, mother and father. . . . Went to St. Joseph's elementary school . . . and I played basketball, I played football. Hangin' out on the corner, chillin' with my friends. You know, just doin' the things, I did all the same things they would do. . . . I was black . . . I was always proud of myself.

The European American student speakers, like Sulli, often referenced their ethnicity as well—signaling insider subject positions in a range of ethnic communities and serving to complicate the "truth" of what it means to be white as well as gay, lesbian, bisexual, or transgendered. Glenda Hennessey, a student speaker who identified as bisexual, often mentioned that she was "the last of eight kids in an Irish Catholic family," and Moe told her audience that her father "grew up in a Jewish family" and noted that he was interested in her finding a "nice Jewish girl" to settle down with.

Once speakers established themselves as insiders to various communities, they told stories that referenced how they internalized heterosexist discourse, positioning themselves as outsiders. As Sulli noted above, he "never told anyone" that he "experimented" with his friend Mark the summer of his eighth grade year. Jamar also recounted how in middle school he never told anyone: "I had a crush on one of my closest friends but I didn't have a word for it. . . . I didn't tell anybody." Similarly, David Anderson, then a junior on the Bureau, told his audiences that in his first year in college he had a relationship with another young man and how after it ended he felt "a little freaked out that I'd been in a relationship with another guy."

Many also had stories of how peers, family members, and others positioned them as outsiders. As Sulli told his audience, he was a sophomore in high school when his priest responded to his gayness by suggesting, "It might be in your best interest to find another place to pray." Often students' parents were the ones who enforced this outsider status. Viany spoke above of how her mother "cried, and she still cries; she hopes I'll get married." Eric Meyer, then a first-year student, told audiences what his father said to him when he was a sophomore in high school:

> He kept me up till 3 A.M. telling me I was immoral, selfish, no one to carry on the family name. He continued with I would get AIDS, telling me how disgusting I was. I was devastated. I didn't want to go on living.

Many times it was peers who reinforced these "truths." Both Moe and Vincente spoke about their experience of being positioned as outsiders for performing the "wrong" gender/sexual identity. Vincente included this story from his middle school years:

> Once my friends were playing around with a makeup compact, so I played with it too, pretending to put makeup on. These four guys came around the corner and said, "You faggot!" That was an awful experience.

These stories of alienation were typically followed by reports of how each student dealt with claiming or being assigned an outsider position. Some students, like Vincente and Jamar, chose to perform heterosexual male identities, to assume insider positions. In his opening story, Vincente clearly told his audience that he knew how to perform social identities valued by the dominant culture when he says, "As a freshman [in high school] I made it my goal to prove to everyone I was straight. By my senior year I had dated a girl for two years, played sports, was class president. Yes! I accomplished it!"

The "truths" in heterosexist discourse would assert that one cannot be "gay" and occupy the valorized social identities of athlete, adolescent male (read heterosexual), and student politician. Vincente introduced a counter-"truth" that "gay people" can occupy, and indeed perform, a number of social identities simultaneously, even when they appear to be conflicting. He used the text of his lived experience to demonstrate how identity itself is multiple, fluid, and performative, complicating what it means to be "gay." Similarly, Jamar told audiences that he made a conscious decision to pass as straight.

> Deep down inside, as much negative information as I received, I never felt bad about myself, powerless over myself. My mama told me never to follow the crowd; she didn't know what she was telling me. . . . I was always very proud of myself. I was black and I knew I was gay, but I didn't tell anybody, but I was always proud of myself.

Others, like Viany, spoke of finding groups like Safe Schools, a program that addressed homophobia in middle and high schools in Massachusetts. This program functioned as a sponsoring institution for Viany, and in high school she joined the group, repositioning herself as an insider.

Some speakers told stories of directly confronting the people who positioned them as outsiders. Eric followed the story about his father with how he summoned a response to his father, a response from his position as an insider to the gay community—a community whose "truths" he was just beginning to internalize: "Then I thought, wait a second, he doesn't understand. I told him so I could be happy and secure in my life." Eric concluded with a story of how he found an ally, a psychologist that at his father's insistence they both went to see. "He [his father] told me, 'Eric, you're going to a psychologist to get "fixed."'" He [the psychologist] told my dad, 'Your son is perfectly normal.' My father went into counseling."

In an act of subversive repetition, Eric's story redefined the word "normal" and the father's homophobia as the "problem." Other speakers explicitly addressed the definition of words, the limits of language, and implicitly the way heterosexist discourse defines the way we understand our lived experiences and those of others. Note that part of the reason Jamar did not "tell anyone" about his crush on another boy was that he didn't know the words to describe his situation and feelings. Similarly, David spoke of his resistance to using words that limited his self-expression. In a Bureau panel, he told his audience with a tone of frustration,

> I think you're all education majors? I've found education majors like labels a lot, so I'll label myself gay. . . . I don't like to say bisexual because right now I'm dating a guy and I'm very much in love with him. But I'm very conscious I'm attracted to women too.

In the same way, Glenda spoke of resisting the associations the term "bisexual" carries when she talked about calling herself a lesbian before identifying as bisexual: "I knew I wasn't a lesbian. I knew I was bisexual, but it was so trendy."

The dialogues that followed these stories created a forum where audience members could grapple with these new, complex identity performances and the notion that the names gay, lesbian, bisexual, and transgendered do not signify a unitary and static identity or position. This allowed audience members to explore and name their own assumptions and stereotypes about the nature of identity, sexuality, and sexual difference.

## Making Allies by Teaching Outlaw "Truths"

The dialogues that followed the opening stories showcased how the Bureau prepared student speakers to perform as effective rhetoricians through their conscious attention to specific identity performance. Dialogues began when the lead speaker invited audience members to ask questions. Katie O'Connor often used this phrase: "I encourage you to ask questions. I'm not afraid of questions." The format of the panel presentations positioned speakers as educators and experts; the questions the audience members posed indicated that they accepted this positioning, though occasionally this position was contested by audience members asserting another "truth" about homosexuality. The dialogue allowed audience members an opportunity not only to recognize the similarities between themselves and the student speakers but also to begin to address and understand the differences—most importantly the difference presented by varying discourses regarding valuing gay people. Through the dialogues, we can see how the speakers used ethos, a variety of discourses, strategies of subversive repetition, and the idea that allies are made, not found, to attempt to change the audience's heterosexist beliefs and attitudes.

Embedded within both the questions of the audience and the responses of the speakers are traces of a variety of discourses. Typically, audience members asked questions about subjects in which they seemed to be genuinely interested, mostly questions concerning family or school life. Other times they asked questions about sexuality or religion or the military or the law. Audience members drew primarily on what they had heard about "gay people" and other minority identities speakers claimed. Mostly they learned these beliefs through heterosexist and other stereotyping discourses in the media and from family and friends, and it was these beliefs they referenced to form their questions. In the following excerpts, we'll see how speakers used appearance and stories and "truths" to connect with and persuade their audiences. At times, speakers did so at the expense of reifying gay identity and heterosexist "truths." In this first example, an audience member asked Vincente about the relationship between his family's ethnicity and his sexuality: "Do you have a big family? How do they deal with it with the Latin community with it being really macho?" The cultural assumptions in this question are that Latinos have big families and that the men are "macho" and therefore homophobic. Vincente says, "If they do find out, it'll be the next big gossip. It'd be a big issue. But I don't care. I have support."

In this case, Vincente confirmed the cultural assumptions. Drawing on his lived experience, he noted that his community and his family would position him as an outsider. However, Vincente went on to assert a counterideology that would read something like, "Though my Latin family is not supportive, gay people have their own supportive communities." Embedded in this cultural ideology is the outlaw discourse typified by phrases from gay political movements such as "Love makes a family" and "Families we choose." Implicitly, Vincente offered audience members a role in this supportive "family" and the idea that a person need not share values with his or her family of origin.

Sometimes audience members asked about cultural norms or laws interanimated by heterosexist discourse. For example, one audience member asked Bob Allen, a man who identified as gay, "Didn't President Clinton just say gay marriage is illegal?" Bob answered by giving factual information about the federal Defense of Marriage Act and detailing the effects of this legislation on survivor benefits, health insurance, and so on. He then gave an example of his own in which he noted that he could not provide these benefit to his male partner of many years, showing the material and personal effects of heterosexist discourse on legal discourse. Doing so confirmed Bob's ethos as an expert and a reliable source.

At times, audience members drew on their own lived experiences. Having heard the opening stories, another audience member asked, "You use the term 'queer.' I always thought it was derogatory?" The cultural assumption here is from heterosexist discourse, that the term is indeed used to stigmatize and warn people and to reinforce the "truth" that "gay people" are perverts, criminals, and the like. Three different speakers as well as an instructor attempted to explain the nuances of outlaw language use:

BOB: It's easier and quicker to say than listing gay, lesbian, bisexual, and transgender. But it does offend a lot of people.

GLENDA: Queer is a generational thing.

MOE: I would much rather be called "dyke" in a nice way than "lesbian" in a nasty way.

INSTRUCTOR: Queer is about reclaiming language. Like young black men call each other "nigger." It takes the power out of the dominant use. Reclaiming a word that's negative from people with societal privilege.

Bob and Glenda drew on their lived experience to explain that queer is a respectful shorthand in some parts of this community but not in others, pointing to the specific differences within the community. Moe also used her lived experience, noting the importance of tone in the use of any word. The instructor added the word "nigger" from racist discourse to give context to the subversive repetition of the words "queer" and "dyke," explaining how all three words are repositioned and valorized in their respective outlaw discourses.

This type of consciousness-raising around word use was explained elegantly by Viany in the interview I had with her. According to Viany, speakers can teach an audience to "maybe understand our language," though she added, "I don't know if we do have a language." Viany listed the words "lipstick lesbian," "dyke," "homosexual," "faggot," and "flaming queen" as examples of gay language and of the differing and specific ways that the community identifies itself. Viany explained that she would tell an audience she might call herself a "lipstick lesbian," but she didn't like the word "dyke" and found the word "homosexual" too medical. By explaining the differences, the nuances of the words, Viany imagined that speakers could help the audience make connections between how the gay community uses words and how words are used in dominant social discourses. Here, Viany was clearly assuming her audience was heterosexually identified, which was not always the case. Viany noted that often audience members asked why homosexuals could call themselves "dykes" or "faggots," but heterosexuals couldn't call them those names. To help audiences understand, Viany said she gave the following example:

'Cause I can call my sister "Spic" and she'd be like, "Shut up," you know. She wouldn't care. But if somebody else called her that, she'd be upset. It's the same thing with "nigger" or any other word. People are kind of learning that. It's a new way people are understanding.

Sometimes a speaker cued a "gay joke" within which was embedded heterosexist discourse in order to demonstrate the effect of these "jokes" on gay people. When an audience member asked David, "Have you ever felt really uncomfortable by a gesture? Has it been really hurtful?" David told this story: "I got into an elevator here [in a dorm] with two other guys and one of them said, 'We have a question. Would you rather sleep with your grandmother or another guy?' Then they laughed." Similarly, to explain homophobia to his audience, Eric also cued a homophobic "joke": "When I was in high school . . . guys would wear T-shirts that said, 'Hey silly faggot, sticks are for chicks.' I went to a homophobic school."

Both Eric and David redefined these "jokes" as homophobic rather than funny, telling them in an act of subversive repetition to re-educate the audience in this outlaw discourse. Eric spoke of how he would like to change his high school, contrasting his experiences there to his experience at the university. When an audience member asked him, "Do you find it hard to go home?" Eric responded,

Every time I go back, I can't stand going back. Maybe we can do a Speaker's Bureau [for Eric's high school]. I'm trying to change the atmosphere from the outside. Here [at the university], I'm able to be exactly who I am.

Here Eric defined himself as someone interested in social change, someone who was comfortably "out" and secure. Jamar and Katie also spoke of themselves as educators, willing to directly confront homophobia.

JAMAR: I would try to educate through my window [when he would hear people calling each other "faggot"]—shout back at them.

KATIE: In the past more than now I try to interrupt it. It's important to be safe too.

Both repositioned themselves from targets of homophobia to agents able to interrupt homophobic speech, though Katie acknowledged that interrupting can be dangerous. These speakers linked the role of educator to performing a risky and important job and in turn linked that to their GLBT identities. Implicitly, they offered their audiences the same opportunity, the same valorized role of an educator accomplishing risky and important work.

Educating others about sexual identity throws into relief religious, medical, and psychological beliefs about the origin of bisexuality/homosexuality. Below is an excerpt in which Moe and Glenda address cultural assumptions about bisexual behavior, specifically beliefs about bisexuality and monogamy and the idea that bisexual people are confused.

AUDIENCE: You said that your mother is bi? If you are bi, is it possible to be married to one or the other?

MOE: My mom is romantic with my dad. It's more that as she grew older, she kind of said, "Women are attractive too." There's no sign that she feels something is missing from her life.

GLENDA: Until you settle down, you stray. Right now I'm in a dating phase; I'm dating as many people as possible. But when I fall in love, I fall in love.

AUDIENCE: Do people think you're confused?

GLENDA: I went through a lot of mental issues, but this is the only issue I'm sure of.

Moe positioned bisexuals as insiders to a community that values monogamy, redefining in the process bisexuality as who you are attracted to rather than who you are actually partnered with. Glenda also drew on her lived experience to explain herself in relation to monogamy as a bisexual woman, inviting her audience through the word "you" to identify with the idea that all people date until they fall in love—a belief her audience probably shared about heterosexuality but not bi- or homosexuality. Bisexuality, she asserted, is

not about confusion at all—even for someone like herself who identified as having "a lot of mental issues."

Below, Katie and Jamar answer some of the most frequently
asked questions that panels received—questions about the origin of
homosexuality:

AUDIENCE: Why are you gay?

KATIE: Mom thinks Dad was a poor role model and that I hung
out with the wrong crowd.

INSTRUCTOR: She thinks you got recruited?

KATIE: Yes. It's about true feelings.

AUDIENCE: Were you born to be gay?

JAMAR: Me, personally, yes. Most parents encourage their kids to
be straight. I knew it wasn't working. I was just trying to
make them happy. From the time I was in elementary school I
knew.

INSTRUCTOR: This is a big question you get asked all the time,
right? Did you choose it, or is it biological?

AUDIENCE: I don't think anyone is born to be gay.

INSTRUCTOR: Did you choose to be straight?

AUDIENCE: I was b— [begins to say "born," then stops short and
begins again]. I believe in the Bible, that people choose to be
gay. Like me, I had no friends but my animals growing up.

INSTRUCTOR: I don't think we're talking about that. You didn't sleep
with your animals.

KATIE: No one knows for sure why people are gay. There's a
danger in saying it's genetic because people will want to "fix"
you or abort unborn children that have a "gay" gene.

Katie began answering this question by cuing psychological
beliefs that lesbians are created by fathers who are poor role models
or by peer pressure in order to contest those notions and asserted
instead her outlaw belief that sexual identity has to do with "true
feelings" or being true to oneself rather than being shaped by exter-
nal forces. Jamar also explained his own understanding of why he
and others are gay by referencing the text of his lived experience,
speaking for himself and asserting an essentialist idea that people are

born gay, though they can pretend otherwise and perform a straight identity. The audience member also cued a text, the Bible, to support the contention that all people are essentially heterosexual and some choose to be gay—implying gayness is related to isolation or a moral shortcoming. This audience member contested the speakers' roles as experts, asserting a counterdiscourse. The instructor in turn challenged the audience member's "truth," and Katie followed, reasserting her expert base by referring to a "truth" from scientific discourse, that "nobody knows" why some people are gay. Here Katie referenced the discourse of eugenics and by association white supremacy as she talked about the danger of the "truth" that being gay is biologically, essentially determined, a kind of genetic flaw, something to "fix." As the instructor noted, this is perhaps one of the most contested "truths" regarding human sexual behavior and identity—is sexual identity essential and fixed or somehow learned and in flux? And further, is there a right and a wrong way to express one's sexual identity?

It is a question that was asked in almost every panel. On another panel, this is how the speakers answered the question, "Do you believe being gay is biologically determined from birth?"

ERIC: All males of my generation are gay on my mom's side. But a lot of people think it's a choice.

VINCENTE: People accuse me, say, "Vincente chooses to be that way." When I was fifteen I would pray every night. I tried really hard. I do feel I was born this way.

KATIE: Definitely for me it wasn't a choice.

Although Eric referenced the aspect of choice in relation to sexual behavior and identity, it is clear that none of the speakers believed that either is socially constructed. All three speakers emphasized, implicitly or explicitly, the essential nature of sexuality, affirming that they did not choose to be gay. They positioned themselves on the one hand as just as "natural" as their heterosexual counterparts, the underlying "truth" being, "It is just as natural for me to be gay as it is for you to be straight." On the other hand, they positioned themselves as victims who could not help who they are or what they do, a cultural ideology drawn from heterosexist discourse that reads something like, "No one would choose to be gay; therefore, it is not possible to choose one's sexual identity." Here, speakers inadvertently positioned themselves as outsiders, never quite "in" enough to be acceptable. They failed to question the heterosexist discourse that positions "gay" as the immutable and unacceptable "other" and instead reproduced the very discourse that subjugated them and their experience.

These identity performances relied upon the perception that homosexuality and integrity contradict each other and that any homosexual who overcomes this contradiction is heroic. This is similar to Eli Clare's idea about how disability and achievement are seen to contradict each other, leaving the disabled to be read as helpless and leading the temporarily-abled to oppress, neglect, and abuse those who are read as disabled (see Clare's "The Mountain"). To believe that integrity contradicts homosexuality is to pair depravity with homosexuality, a pairing for which those identified as GLBT pay an awful price. By positioning themselves as heroic and unusual, these speakers created a new and static identity for "good gays" that are "just like us." This notion is an appealing one and, indeed, appeals to audiences.

When one instructor called for appreciative feedback from the class for the speakers, the responses one audience member gave indicated how appealing the above "truth" is to her:

> I think just because you are both [Vincente and Viany] so close to our age and you're both beautiful people, it helps me to understand. You didn't try to be anyone but yourselves. You're just like us. Helps me differentiate that the only difference is who you love, and it doesn't matter if they're male or female.

This young woman of color took up the ally role offered by the speakers and tried out an ideology new to her, "gay people are just like us." Though this new ideology did not address the "heroic-gay" conundrum, it did build a bridge of identification and, I think, met to an extent her need to understand the situation homophobia creates for gay people. In an interview after this presentation, I learned more about the ethos these speakers wanted to present and what went into their performance of identities where they were read as "just like us." Viany told me how she and Vincente talked about presenting themselves for this particular class, a diversity class earmarked as a people of color section. They dressed carefully for their peers, mirroring the styles for young Puerto Rican women and men, a detail noted not only by the woman above but also by a young black man in the audience who said,

> I'm not the most open person about sexuality. But by bringing it closer to me it makes it less of a mystery, know what I'm sayin'? And Vincente, I seen you around all the time and you dress impeccably [laughter from both speakers and audience].

This young man seemed to be connecting with the speakers and the outlaw discourse through a subversive repetition, referencing the cultural ideology that gay men are smart dressers and crossing a gender norm by commenting on another man's appearance. By taking up the ally position offered to him, the audience member took the opportunity to perform an identity new to him—a young heterosexual man of color willing to appreciate and compliment a young gay man of color.

None of the "truths" offered above addressed the hierarchy based on sexual difference and how it might be transformed. The speakers did not ask the audience to consider how it is that some differences are deemed "good and natural" and others "bad and unnatural." Refusing to see differences or marking differences as "good" or "bad" essential identities reifies the hierarchy. Some speakers did attempt to address this situation. In this same panel, Christa Ferriera, who identified as a heterosexual ally, talked about how she was attempting to acknowledge sexual differences as simply another difference to learn about. Christa pointed to the importance of language use in maintaining a hierarchy based on sexual difference, modeling how a person might use language to act as an ally.

Recently I've been making more attempts to use non-heterosexual terms. I wouldn't say I'm a perfect ally; I have issues too. But I do think that learning about it, you learn
about differences. It's easier to accept.

Christa made a link between becoming an ally and attempting
to use "non-heterosexual terms," using language to make visible the
fact that not everyone identifies as heterosexual. She linked learning about and acknowledging the differences between herself and
those identified as GLBT to becoming an ally. She offered, implicitly, audience members an ally role to play that included acceptance
of differences without having to be "perfect" or free of "issues."
    Shane Phelan notes that we cannot afford to ignore differences,
nor do GLBT people need to claim they were "born that way," but
rather must acknowledge that some folks feel they were born into
an identity and others freely "converted" or chose to become GLBT
and that all people are human and complicated. By definition, GLBT
people are human and have basic human needs for justice, safety,
community, and love. In a truly democratic society, citizens strategize
together so that all citizens can have those needs met. By performing identities that were recognizably "human and complicated," these
student speakers helped audiences see and identify with the basic
human needs the speakers had that were unmet by the network of
customs and laws that define non-heterosexual expressions and partnerships as non-human, deviant, and monolithic. Speakers' stories
clarified what these customs and laws are and introduced "truths"
from the outlaw discourse, which provided the audience with a new
ideological frame of reference. When ally speakers also shared their
own process of learning about these new "truths" and of respecting
the real and specific differences between themselves and their GLBT
allies, audiences were introduced to the idea that we need not be all
the same in order to treat each other equitably, that we need not
maintain hierarchies based on sexual difference. Linking the words
used to vilify GLBT folks with those words used to stigmatize black
and Latinos implicitly showed the parallels between hierarchies based
on sexuality and those based on race/ethnicity.

The work student speakers did in connection with the Bureau clearly facilitated their rhetorical growth through conscious attention to specific identity performance. The role of the Bureau as a sponsoring institution—offering the structure and content—provides us an example of the key elements we as writing teachers might adapt to our own classrooms. In the next two chapters, I'll talk more about how we might make these links explicit in the classroom.

In the next chapter, I examine how conscious attention to specific identity performance can facilitate crossover effect, the ability of writers to transfer rhetorical development in one context to other contexts. We'll see in two case studies how Vincente and Moe performed their identities in order to move audiences, not only as speakers on the Bureau but also as students in classrooms and citizens in the larger community.

# 3 / Negotiating Multiplicities: Performing Identities in Context

> I feel like I have two stories here. . . . I try to choose what will
> make more sense to the audience and tell the story that people
> can relate to.
>
> —Vincente Colon

**T**eaching writing in one context in a way that crosses over to success in another context is a discipline-wide concern. The immediate problem for many of our students is how to move from writing for evaluation within the protected walls of the academy to writing for rhetorical accomplishment in the community. There are many examples in community service–learning literature of the problem of trying to transfer rhetorical knowledge from school to other settings in the community. Nora Bacon, Linda Flower, Thomas Deans, and other community service–learning scholars note the difficulty students have in making this transfer. Nor is this sort of transfer problem confined to moving from rhetorical knowledge in school to rhetorical accomplishment in community projects. Paul Prior notes the difficulty first-year graduate students have as they are acculturated into the rhetoric of graduate school and begin to reposition themselves as graduate students. Many in composition studies believe first-year college students also struggle with discourse-related transfer problems as they move from high schools and cultures that do not necessarily match with the white, middle-class discourses valued in colleges and universities (see Newkirk; Fox, "Basic Writing"; and Bartholomae and Petrosky). And of course, proficiency in the rhetoric of first-year college writing classes does not guarantee rhetorical success in the context of other disciplines in the academy. The advent of writing across the curriculum initiatives speaks to this observation.

YES!

Tom Deans notes the importance of distinguishing writing *about* communities or community issues in school from writing *for* or *with* communities to address community issues. In his book *Writing Partnerships: Service-Learning in Composition,* Deans emphasizes the necessity of teaching the explicit rhetoric for each of these contexts. According to Deans, each paradigm or context (for, about, with) values a specific discourse that in turn offers students particular roles. Simply put, writing *about* the community engages students in academic discourse about the community service work they have done, positioning students as academic writers in the classroom. Writing *for* the community positions students as novice professional writers who use workplace discourse to create needed professional documents for agencies that serve various communities; the most common of these documents are pamphlets, training manuals, grant proposals, and reports. Writing *with* the community asks students to collaborate directly with community members in a relationship unmediated by an agency. In this sort of writing, students share the role of writer and expert with their community partners and develop a hybrid discourse composed of academic and community discourses to collaboratively identify and address local problems (17).

Implicit in Deans's argument is a focus on ethos and how these varying community discourses shape ethos. Deans asks us to consider how each community context calls for a particular rhetoric we must consider as we guide our students to succeed in community writing projects. However, Deans does not explicitly ask us to consider how we might teach students the connection between ethos, identity as performance, and the ground—the discourses that shape ethos—a connection I contend is necessary for students to understand if they are to successfully transfer their rhetorical knowledge across contexts.

In "The Trouble with Transfer: Lessons from a Study of Community Service Writing," Nora Bacon documents the difficulties that students at San Francisco State University have as they move from writing in school to writing for community projects. As Bacon explores the relationship between the school-based rhetorical knowledge students have and the rhetorical knowledge students need to succeed when they write for community-based organizations, she notes eight important factors. At the top of this list is student knowledge about writing, which includes their theories of writing, students' view of themselves as writers, and their rhetorical awareness. She notes that one key to students' success in writing for the community is their awareness of the social dimensions of writing for community-based agencies. By social dimensions, Bacon means the roles students are offered in the social context of community-based agencies or are able to create for themselves. Bacon draws attention to two areas that are germane to specific identity performance: students' view of themselves as writers and the social dimensions of students' experience. Like Deans, Bacon emphasizes how writing in community contexts can assist students in creating new identities for themselves that contribute to their own rhetorical successes as well as to community needs. Absent from Bacon's analysis is the consideration of how this happens, a gap I hope to address with my theory of specific identity performance.

"How do you talk effectively across the boundaries of knowledge, values, and cultural background?" (Flower 16). This is one of the first questions Linda Flower asks students who will be writing with communities whose knowledge, values, and cultural backgrounds are different from their own. This question is at the center of my own work and is the implicit question student speakers ask themselves each time they enter a classroom to address the community problem of homophobia and heterosexism and attempt to build new knowledge with their peers about what it might mean to be "gay." In Flower's textbook *Problem-Solving Strategies for Writing in College and Community,* she advises her students to first remember that they are already part of many different communities. She points out to students that they already know something about speaking across discourse boundaries and suggests that they make this knowledge conscious in order to learn how to write with communities. In order to address and solve community problems with community members, Flower tells students that they "must learn to talk as if you [they] belong" (16). Indeed, this is the solution student speakers have also hit upon; they reference themselves as insiders: students

with recognizable majors who are familiar with campus cultur
are a part of it. Student speakers address their peers in an attempt to
"write" a new knowledge about "gay" people with them. Whereas
Flower's strategies for assisting students to write in new rhetorical
situations hinges on identifying "shared goals" (208) and learning
the rhetorical ways of the communities with which they wish to write,
she leaves out what I see as a crucial step: learning about specific identity performance.

Students who write about, for, or with communities are not the
only students who grapple with differing discourse communities.
Writing across the curriculum initiatives have become important pre-
cisely because the primary task of undergraduate college students is
to learn how to write in many different discipline-specific discourses
in order to fulfill bachelor degree requirements. Writing across the
curriculum has challenged the notion that first-year composition
courses can teach students what they need to know to write in discipline-specific discourses. Implementing cross-disciplinary study
groups has enabled faculty to begin to articulate common rhetorical
ground across the curriculum and to identify discipline-specific
rhetoric that may best be taught in junior-year writing courses in each
major. Although the task of graduate students differs from that of undergraduates in terms of which discourse communities they must
learn to negotiate, they too must learn to write and speak across discourse communities. In his studies of graduate students, Paul Prior
posits that they assume multiple stances in "the different systems of
graduate schools, the department, advisors and committees, graduate student employment, and the job market" ("Literate Activity" 277).

Because these multiple systems or discourse communities exist
simultaneously, moving from the background to the foreground, graduate students must learn to change their footings continuously. I propose that we can better teach the rhetoric of these various discourses
by explicitly teaching students to become conscious of the specific
identities they are performing and of how those performances are necessarily shaped by the discourses within which they play their roles.

Thus the conundrum for mainstream college students includes
how to write for different teachers or in different disciplines and also

how to transfer the rhetorical knowledge they've acquired in school to rhetorical accomplishment in writing *for* and *with* communities outside of the academy. In this book, I look specifically at how we as teachers of first-year writing can foster the sort of rhetorical growth in all students that does assist them in making transfers across rhetorical contexts by examining how student speakers on the Speaker's Bureau do so.

It seems that understanding the rhetorical work of specific identity performances assists student speakers on the Bureau to make the sort of rhetorical transfers across contexts we want all students to learn to make. Those students who have the experience of speaking for the Bureau seem to more easily make these transfers. The quote with which I begin this chapter is an example from Vincente of the sort of rhetorical savvy, the conscious shifts, an accomplished rhetor chooses to make in relation to audience. Vincente told me in his second interview that he did indeed have more than one story about coming out to his mother and described how and why he chose to tell which story to his peers at Bureau panel presentations and which to tell to the invisible audience of his writing placement exam. In part, Vincente and the other speakers who identified as gay were more able to wrestle effectively with rhetorical transfers across contexts because the task was not new to them. Gay students have the experience of crafting and performing multiple identities in ways students who are positioned by the dominant discourses as central rather than marginal simply do not.

Assessing the prevailing discourses and the likely material consequences of discourses like homophobia or racism is something that those who are positioned as marginal by their race, ethnicity, and/or sexuality (and other marginalized identities) simply do consciously as a survival strategy. Students who are positioned as marginal are aware that certain identity performances are valorized and often choose to perform those identities for their own personal safety. Mainstream students who are by definition positioned as central rather than marginal grow up in a very different context. Though some of their identities may be more or less dominant, typically those who are positioned as "white" and "straight" and "male" are those who are less likely to have had the experience of needing to assess discourses and their possibly dangerous material consequences consciously in order to perform identities for their personal safety.

Intersectionality plays a large role in this process. In the case studies that follow, we can see how student speakers consciously claimed and spoke from their multiple identities as well as resisted how prevailing discourses attempted to construct them. Each speaker's body was the nexus for a variety of identities (race, class, gender, and, of course, sexuality). Speakers had the opportunity to finely tune their already well-developed sense of audience and context when they participated in Bureau training workshops, meetings, and panel presentations. The implicit focus on specific identity performance on the Bureau highlighted for speakers how their choices of which identities to claim/hide/spin depended on the context and audience receiving the performance.

In the previous chapters, I have discussed how student speakers crafted various specific identity performances for different contexts. In this chapter, we can see, through interviews with Vincente and Moe, that student speakers were self-aware and able to articulate the reasons behind the rhetorical work they were accomplishing. Student speakers on the Speaker's Bureau carefully selected the stories they told about themselves on panel presentations, using these stories to create specific identity performances that invited their audiences to become allies. Rather than focus only on similarities or only on differences between themselves and their audiences, speakers instead wove the specific threads of similarities and differences between themselves and their audiences, complicating what it means to "be gay." Positioned by the forum of the Bureau as experts and educators, speakers used these stories to lead their peers to question the "truths" of normative social discourses, most especially heterosexist discourse that stigmatizes, pathologizes, and criminalizes those identified as gay. Speakers introduced alternative "truths" from an outlaw discourse and attempted to recast "gay people" as human and complicated, possessing the same human needs for justice, community, and love as the audience members with whom they spoke.

In this chapter, I examine the work the Speaker's Bureau participants did in writing as well as in speaking as they performed identities both inside and outside the classroom. I show how the same individual student speaker created different performances of identity in different settings and was aware (in interviews with me) of the intentional shaping of those performances. Through examples of the same speaker doing multiple performances of identity, we will see the slightly different identity constructions and how they are linked to student speakers' different senses of audience. This chapter is a bridge, linking the rhetorical identity performances of student speakers to the writing of students in our classes.

## The Case Studies

Vincente and Moe provided me with a number of written pieces, representing, between them, the range of writing I collected from student speakers. Each of these students had a unique relationship to writing, also representing the range of relationships to writing I observed in the other student speakers. In an interview, Vincente told me that he was not drawn to writing, nor did he read very often, preferring dance and theater to express himself. Vincente's discomfort with reading and writing seemed related to his ease of expression as a dancer and an actor and perhaps to the fact that English was not his first language. Unlike Vincente, Moe had a long and successful history of reading and writing for school, for newspapers, and for herself. Moe's facility with reading and writing seemed in large part attributable to her own preferences as well as to the mentoring and role modeling she received from her family and the leader of a youth support group she joined as a junior in high school.

In each case study, I first examine Bureau presentations and contrast those with the rhetorical constructions each created for class assignments. I end each case study by looking at how Vincente and Moe constructed themselves in public anonymous writing as well as in private writing.

### Vincente Colon

Vincente was a third-year sophomore when I interviewed him the first time; it was his second semester on the Bureau as a gay male speaker. He learned about the Bureau when a friend invited him to sit in and observe a presentation. By joining the Bureau, Vincente hoped to address stereotypes against gay people; in particular he wanted to reach Puerto Rican/Spanish and black youth. The Bureau's emphasis on becoming an educator to change heterosexist attitudes appealed to Vincente, and he told me that joining the Bureau helped him to come out of the closet. Here we can see the role of a sponsoring institution like the Bureau in assisting Vincente to create a new identity for himself as an out-of-the-closet educator.

In this first interview, I learned that Vincente was aware of the normative gender performances for men and women and how those legal performances contrasted with his own gender performances. He told me that the men in his neighborhood "had to be very macho. . . . A man has to be a man, a woman a woman." In his second interview with me, Vincente elaborated on the way heterosexist discourse worked to position gay men in his neighborhood as "really, really feminine—a raving queen dressed in drag. White and dirty. Morally dirty—likes children—dresses funny, dresses in pink."

Vincente recalled for me how his father "was always hassling" him about the way he spoke. "He told me to quit stressing my s's so much," something Vincente told me his father associated with effeminate behavior. Before Vincente was in junior high school, he was aware that part of the legal performance of gender for boys was romantic/sexual interest in girls, a norm he told me he had transgressed with another boy his age. "We were best friends and we ended up hooking up one day. I don't remember how it all happened, but I realized I couldn't tell anybody, 'cause it was weird, but for me it seemed pretty normal."

The discourses in Vincente's neighborhood constructed same-sex attraction as "morally dirty," "feminine," and "white"—all stigmatized as abnormal for a Puerto Rican boy. In the face of these normative social discourses, Vincente reported in retrospect that he constructed himself privately as "pretty normal" until junior high school. Following is a quote Vincente often related on Bureau panels, a quote I referenced in chapters 1 and 2. In this quote, we can see how Vincente first invited his audience to recall their own outsider positions in junior high—tacitly inviting the audience into the role of outsider, an outsider who may have also performed a role for survival in school. We can see here how Vincente internalized the way heterosexist/sexist discourses position boys who are attracted to boys and who stress their s's as feminine and how in high school Vincente reconstructed himself as masculine to conform to the legal gender performances for men:

> How many people enjoyed junior high? No one? Maybe a few. Everyone always teases. When I was younger, I had feminine characteristics. Once my friends were playing around with a makeup compact, so I played with it too, pretending to put makeup on. These four guys came around the corner and said, "You faggot!" That was an awful experience. As a freshman [in high school] I made it my goal to prove to everyone I was straight. By my senior year I had dated a girl for two years, played sports, was class president. Yes! I accomplished it!

This excerpt emphasizes Judith Butler's idea that we construct and perform our various rhetorical identities intentionally as a survival strategy within social discourses that essentially determine and govern that performance. Vincente told his audience that he created a "straight" identity performance for his high school peers and succeeded in performing that role. Vincente's relationship to the audience for the Bureau presentation was that of a guest expert and educator, though the audience was composed of other college students like himself.

He also told this story about coming out to his mother:

> October 9th I went to a Speaker's Bureau meeting. On October 10th I told my mom. . . . It's just the two of us; my father passed away two years ago next month. I told her, "I'm gay." She just sat there, then started to cry and ask, "Where did I go wrong?" I told her, "Nothing, there's no big reason why."

Here he invited the audience to identify with him as an insider, someone with a mom who worried about him and her role in the person he turned out to be. Though his mother's question positioned gay people and their parents as somehow guilty of doing something wrong, Vincente's answer positioned both himself and his mother as innocent of any wrongdoing.

In our second interview, I asked Vincente why he chose to tell these particular stories to Bureau audiences, and he told me, "I know that it's what works with the audience." Later in the same interview, Vincente stressed again the importance of choosing to tell these stories:

> I try to choose what will make more sense to the audience and . . . tell the story that people can also relate to. . . . How I tell my story is more on a down-to-earth level, where we're kinda sorta on the same plane.

We had been discussing other stories Vincente had told to other audiences, stories he regarded as "messy." When I noted to him that we human beings are necessarily complicated and "messy," Vincente laughed and responded, "I don't want to leave them thinking, 'Gay people are just messy.' I don't want them to know how messy we can be."

Vincente used particular stories to create an ethos he believed his audience would understand, a persona with whom they could relate, steering clear of stories that might compound stereotypes about gay men. He told audiences that he liked to watch sports and to dance and happened to be gay, preferring to construct himself as "down-to-earth . . . not so far from you," a man who did not try to transgress legal gender performances.

Another public venue in which Vincente constructed himself as "down-to-earth" was the writing classroom. At the time of our first interview, Vincente composed an essay about the misrepresentation of gay men for his first-year writing course, which was a small, twenty-four-person workshop where peer review and personal essays were the norm. As a sophomore, Vincente was older than most of his classmates, a position that garnered him some expert currency. The instructor of this class was a man Vincente knew to be a colleague and friend of mine. These factors enabled Vincente to write about his experience as a gay man, and it was in fact one of the few essays he completed before he dropped the class. He told me how surprised he was as he began this essay, despite his long-standing anxiety about writing: "I always struggle with the beginning and end [of essays], and, like, it [this essay] just flowed to me. You know, all that was in my head, and I just started writing all that down." Apparently the topic of representation together with the role he had assumed on the Bureau as an educator made it possible for Vincente to reconstruct himself as someone who could write with ease, someone who had something important to say. Vincente titled his piece "Please, Don't Make Me into a Hairdresser" and began with these assertions:

> No, I don't like listening to ABBA, I don't like to dress in drag. . . . Yes, I am a gay male. Confused? Let me confuse you some more. Yes, I like basketball and football, I own all the Jackie Chan movies. Now you're thinking, "Wait, that's impossible, you can't be gay."

He went on to encourage his audience to ask themselves why they are confused and to suggest that the confusion stems from the way "gay men are represented in today's culture. . . . Our society thinks we're supposed to be flaming queens." Here Vincente constructed a "we" of gay men who do not adhere to the stereotypes, a counter to the "we" who do and are stigmatized, simultaneously complicating who gay men are and creating a hierarchy of "normal" versus "stereotypical" gay men. Vincente followed this suggestion with another question, "Why do you suppose everyone has this mentality?," and explained to his audience, "We're born and one of the first things we see is mommy and daddy." Here the "we" he created was a role he offered to share with his audience—the "we" that learns what is "normal" at home and learns to reinforce that norm by stigmatizing those who don't fit in at school. "We start to make fun of anything that isn't, whether one is overweight, a person of color, or wears glasses."

Vincente moved next to describe what it was like for him to be a "gay Latino male."

> People in Latino and Black communities assume that no one in the neighborhood can be gay because of the way we're suppose to act as "macho" men. Anyone who is a man must act

like a man. Homosexuality is something that isn't mentioned
in my neighborhood . . . almost forbidden.

In response to these rules about gender performances for men, Vincente noted that he "didn't have any problems . . . because I was
forced to be 'in the closet'" and was "too busy playing the straight
role." He wrote that "my role changed" when he arrived at the university because the university culture was a place "where people start
thinking for themselves and start questioning, 'Well, what is "normal" anyway?'" Here Vincente suggested yet another role for his audience, that of "more open-minded" folks who are able and willing
to question what is the normal or legal performance of gender, for
men in particular. Vincente linked this open-mindedness to the number of gay characters on TV, then ended his essay with two points:
first, that the "consequences" of learning that being gay is "not right"
can lead students to "become mentally unstable or . . . commit suicide," and second, that "more awareness" will lead people, he hoped,
to "see that we're not all hairdressers."

Vincente's identity performance as a member of a writer's workshop for the first-year writing class was substantially the same as his
performance as a Bureau speaker. He represented himself as a young
man who had little difficulty coming to terms with his sexuality,
though he implied this would not have been the case had he come
out in his neighborhood instead of the relatively liberal university.
Both performances underscored the pressure of heterosexist discourse and Vincente's facility at playing "the straight role" to fit in
until he could find a community with a counter-discourse. Vincente
took on the role of educator in both instances, using references to
insider and outsider roles and inviting his audience to occupy the
role of ally he created for them.

Unlike his performance in the Bureau presentations, the forum
of the essay seemed to allow Vincente the space to explain how stereotypes and oppressive norms are maintained—what we learn at
home and what gets reinforced at school. In this essay, Vincente was
able to clearly lead his audience to consider "What is normal anyway?"
and to tie this question to the mission of the university, the goal of a
university education, to think for yourself. Vincente offered his au-

dience a choice: perpetuate stereotypes and norms that oppress gay people in particular, or break the cycle of oppression.

Notably, Vincente did not explicitly question the sexist/misogynist discourse that positions gay men who *are* hairdressers as "other," as "not right." However, he did reference the "macho" role men in "Latino and Black communities" must play, noting that the representation of gay men in "Hispanic culture is . . . a little harsher than in others." In both instances, Vincente did imply that "real gay men" are substantially the same as "real men"—they like sports and violent movies too and, as Vincente says, "happen to be gay."

Though in these public performances, Vincente suggested only the faintest connections between oppressive discourses, Vincente told me in his second interview with me that he had recently realized how "discrimination" affected his experience in the Latino and gay communities:

> I can't be gay because my culture doesn't let me be gay; my culture doesn't allow me to be who I want to be. If I'm in the gay community, there's not many people of color around, and it's very into the gay culture, so I can't really be my culture either. I have to like Madonna and that type of thing.

Vincente spoke clearly of the unsatisfying choices with which he was faced:

> You either choose to stay in your own culture and remain closeted, or you kind of decide to do the gay culture and you kind of lose your heritage and your old culture, 'cause you can't have both things at once. And that's really unfortunate. I've lost a lot of my Spanish culture.

In these excerpts, Vincente spoke of yet other roles he performed in order to fit in—that of a straight Spanish man and that of a gay Spanish man who assimilated to the gay white culture. Here Vincente connected the effects of racist and heterosexist discourses as they converged in two audiences he found himself "playing" for: a straight Spanish audience and a gay white audience. Vincente did reference one evening at a gay club on "Latin Night" when he was able to perform an identity that seemed organically more complete to him: a gay Spanish man. Though Vincente was aware that this particular audience existed only for a fleeting moment, noting that he was certain that most Latinos who attended this club were closeted, he told me:

> I always wanted to know what it was like to dance merengue and salsa with another guy. I just thought it would be so cool. And for the first time, going out with them . . . felt so right and I felt so at home.

Like the interviews, the anonymous and private writing that Vincente did created a space, an audience for whom Vincente could construct a more complicated identity for himself and thus imagine how he might invite a more complicated and nuanced audience, a community of allies, into being.

The university writing placement test, a large public exam that provided anonymity to the test-takers, granted Vincente the opportunity to create such an audience. By the time I read his writing placement exam, Vincente and I had been in Bureau workshops together and had presented our stories on panels as co-speakers for a little over a year. We had an easy camaraderie and a genuine appreciation of the work we did together on the Bureau. At the time, I was coordinating the administration and reading of these exams, and I noted as I read Vincente's essay that he had written about coming out to his mother in response to the exam prompt "What has helped you or forced you to grow up and mature?" I had heard Vincente's coming out story many times by then and in different contexts: in Bureau workshops, in Bureau presentations, and in the first interview we had. Vincente had told the same basic story each time: telling his mother in October 1996, his mother crying and asking what she had done "wrong," and Vincente reassuring her that she had done nothing wrong, that there was "no big reason" why he was gay.

In contrast, the essay Vincente wrote described how he had come out to his mother in the summer of 1995. Clearly, this was a different story:

> Summer and Fall of '95 was definitely the most challenging period in my life, causing me to mature and grow-up. In the Summer of '95 I had come out to my mother about my sexuality. I felt it was about time to be open about my sexuality due to the fact I've been oppressed for so many years. Typically, like most parents, my mother did not take this well. I asked her to not let anyone know until I was more prepared. I had especially asked her to not let my father know, because at the time he was terminally ill. She concurred.
>
> Fall of '95 came and within two weeks of being in school my father passed away. This caused much stress in my life. For it was after my father passed away my mother decided to cut off all ties with her only child. This caused me great hardship because I was then alone with no family or friends to turn to. I had to leave school because of the stress. I found a job and worked hard enough to make enough money to support myself. I was then able to come back to school to further my education. What I have learned from this experience is that no one is going to hand anything to you. If you want something or need help, you need to go out and get it yourself. In the long run, I think what has happened with my coming out to my mother and [her] cutting off all ties with [me] is o.k. When I'm successful, I can look back and say "I did it, and there is no one that can throw anything in my face."
>
> To me being "grown up" or "mature" is all about learning and experiencing. Without the willing [sic] to do both, the real world will almost force you to grow up one way or the other. I felt like I was almost forced. If I didn't go ahead with the force, then I could have either been in jail, out in the streets hustling (doing whatever necessary to survive)

or worse [*sic*] case scenario . . . I would have been dead. Thankfully, I headed in the right direction. With these experiences I feel that I am now a responsible and mature individual.

As I read Vincente's exam, I realized I wanted to understand what it was like for him to take the exam and how he decided to tell this particular story. When he and I met for our second interview about the exam, he expressed surprise that I had read it, saying,

Once you just put a lid on it—especially something on a sheet of paper—you think it's going to be tossed away, not come back a couple years later. When you write it you don't know who's on the other end reading it. . . . And you're okay with that . . . 'cause you're never going to see that person.

Vincente went on to say that even if he had worked with a teacher for a whole semester, he would never have written this story for a class. Despite that, Vincente told me, "I'm definitely okay with you using it," and expressed how relieved he was to have a chance to explain the differences between the coming out story in the exam and the coming out story he told publicly—particularly because he felt worried that I couldn't understand without his explanations that both stories were indeed true.

When I asked Vincente what it was like to take this exam and what made him decide to tell the story, he answered without hesitation, "This was just a huge turning point in my life . . . a time in my life where I had no choice but to be responsible or otherwise it would . . . turn out in a really bad way." He went on to explain how he wrote the essay:

I just remember sitting back for a second and thinking, "Well, I have to really be honest, not bullshit." I closed my eyes and I thought . . . "What's brought me to where I am now? And what makes me want to be honest?" And then I just started writing.

When I asked why it was he didn't share this version of his coming out story publicly, he told me, "I feel like I have two stories here," and the one he chose to tell in public was "much better for me to talk about, much easier for me to talk about than what's on the other side of the fence." As we continued to discuss the story in the exam, Vincente noted that when people asked him about his father he would tell them, "Yeah, he passed away," and if they asked how, he would reply, "He had AIDS," but he told me he rarely ever tells anyone what happened after his father died: "Yeah, we got evicted . . . my mom disowned me." Vincente said he never talked about how both his parents were IV drug users and that due to his mother's addiction, they were evicted from their home after his father's death. He didn't want to explain that when his mother recovered and they reconnected, she "acted as if nothing ever happened and I had to go through the process [coming out] again." It was this second coming out that Vincente storied for his public audiences, where his mother cries and asks why and Vincente also acts "as if nothing ever happened," as if this was the first and only time he has come out to his mother.

Vincente told me he chose to forget the story he told in the exam, this part of his life, what he called "the other side of me," and "block it out as much as I can." He said he believed that telling the exam story would give the impression that "gay people are just messy," not "down-to-earth," the identity construction he wanted to perform for his audiences.

Vincente's reflections on the exam story show how aware he was of the prevailing social discourses of moralistic judgment—a discourse that would, for example, construct IV drug users as bad people and Puerto Ricans as irresponsible parents. The discourse of moralistic judgment constructs "good" and "bad" people and perpetuates the notion that punishments are "deserved" by those who are bad people or act like bad people. Telling the exam story publicly would put Vincente and his family in the position of being judged, since in moralistic discourse there are only two uncomplicated positions to occupy: good or bad. Vincente knew that "drug addict," "Puerto Rican," and "gay" are most often constructed as bad in moralistic discourse and chose to simplify his story to construct a good "gay-boy-next-door" identity from a "nice" family.

The anonymous audience that Vincente constructed for the exam, on the other hand, apparently invited the "messy-ness" of Vincente's life. It seems that if he was to claim the identity of a "mature" and "grown up" person, this audience needed to know and understand the very stories Vincente excluded from his public performances. Vincente constructed a gay identity for the audience of the exam, one that had been hidden and oppressed and was further isolated by his mother's reactions and actions. In this story, Vincente, as the disowned young gay man, acknowledged the social forces that shape the experience of many young people in his position and the possible consequences: "I could have either been in jail, out in the streets hustling (doing whatever necessary to survive) or worse [*sic*] case scenario . . . I would have been dead." He also constructed himself as an actor, describing the consequences of his ability to take action:

> I found a job and worked hard enough to make enough
> money to support myself. I was then able to come back to
> school to further my education. . . . Thankfully, I headed in
> the right direction. With these experiences I feel I am now
> a responsible and mature individual.

Vincente also invoked a familiar American "self-made man" role as he made sense of how coming out to his mother resulted in her disowning him, saying, "When I'm successful, I can look back and say 'I did it, and there is no one that can throw anything in my face.'" This audience, unlike the public audiences Vincente addressed, does not need to be persuaded that gay people are okay and that homophobia is unnecessary; that is not the purpose of this piece. Nonetheless, Vincente did not exclude his gay identity, and in fact, the discourse of heterosexism is clearly at work, shaping the circumstances in the exam story.

Vincente connected the writing he did for the placement exam with his writing in a very private venue, his journal. In the excerpt below, Vincente begins by talking about his exam, the audience for the exam, and then the audience for his journal:

> Along with me being honest about it [what forced him to
> grow up], at the same time I think I just wanted some kind

of attention and wanted . . . somebody to listen to me. It's not so much . . . the person that's reading it, but how, like my journal. For me, my journal is my best listener.

Here the journal itself was the audience, and like the anonymous audience of the exam, this audience was apparently compassionate: "It doesn't give me any kind of horrible feedback. I can tell my journal whatever I want, and it's okay, no matter how dumb or silly or emotional or mean I can be. And he listens to me." Clearly the journal (personified as "he") empathetically listened to a variety of performances from Vincente—Vincente as mean, as silly, as dumb—performances of himself he did not share with any other audience. Indeed, the fear of someone else discovering his journal or other private writing often caused him to either throw away or code his private writing. Vincente remembered composing and then throwing away a suicide note he wrote as a teenager in regard to the stress of keeping his sexuality hidden as well as other "pressures" he didn't explain. It was around this time he started and then stopped keeping a journal, fearful his parents would discover it. In college, he resumed keeping a journal, coding his references—switching pronouns from "he" to "she" and names from "Michael" to "Michele"—for fear of his roommate discovering the journal. Vincente constructed the possible secondary audience of his private writing as the people around him—folks who were not entirely friendly or at least quite comfortable with homosexuality. It was this audience that Vincente continued to address in his most public writing.

### Moe Pontiack

Moe, who was a junior when I interviewed her, began speaking on the Bureau as a first-year student because, as she told me, "I really, really wanted to come out after so long being in the closet. The more chances, the better." As I noted in chapter 2, Moe believed that speaking on the Bureau was "the most effective way to educate people about gay and lesbian issues," and she positioned herself as an out lesbian educator to do so. The name Moe Pontiack is a pseudonym Moe chose for herself as a teenager, and it is the pseudonym she asked me to use for her in this book. She began to use the name when she wrote her first letters to the editor of the local newspaper, explaining the oppressive circumstances of her life as a closeted lesbian teenager. She selected the name Moe because it was, in her words, "the butchiest thing" she could come up with. Moe told me she was tired of people "trying to get me to be more femme, and if I was gonna pick a name, it was gonna be butch. I just felt more comfortable. Also, like, more rebellious."

Moe used her given name, a decidedly feminine name, on Bureau presentations and for all her class work; however, for anonymous writing and other anonymous contributions, like this study, she constructed a "butch" and "rebellious" identity. This identity was not far from the way Moe performed her identity in the world through the way she dressed and moved and spoke. Moe wore jeans, T-shirts, and flannels with boots or sneakers and certainly did not move or speak in stereotypically feminine ways. When as a child Moe rebelled and refused to wear dresses to religious services, unlike her twin sister, she realized she was doing something "wrong" according to the "truths" of moralistic and heterosexist/sexist discourse. This sense of "wrongness" around the way Moe performed her gender deepened for her in sixth and seventh grade when, as I noted in the previous chapter, she became the target of her classmates' reproduction and instantiation of these discourses: "My classmates decided I was a lesbian. Funny, 'cause I hadn't yet."

Like many people, those around her conflated her illegal gender performances with her sexuality, one signifying the other; her gender nonconformity disturbed the naturalized hegemony of men over women. Like Vincente, Moe understood early on the legal gender performances for men and women, girls and boys. When Moe was fifteen, she realized that she was in love with her friend, another girl her age. So fully had Moe internalized the "truths" of compulsory heterosexuality and gender hierarchy that she remembered saying to herself, "I can't be a lesbian because . . . I didn't wear leather, and . . . I didn't live in New York City. And like, you know, I was me— I wasn't like, this stranger."

Moe realized, rightly, that she was not performing what she had learned was a lesbian: a leather-wearing, big-city stranger. The following year, Moe discovered the book *Patience and Sarah* by Isabel

Miller while searching the local college library for information about lesbians. The book, she told me, became her "bible" because the author described the two young women in the book as "young, strong, and unashamed of their relationship" and "they [Patience and Sarah] had normal thoughts." The absence of the words "gay" or "lesbian" reassured Moe, who had learned to associate homosexuality with the themes of "dying" and "AIDS" and "promiscuity," themes she did not find in the book. Moe told me, "It wasn't a book about lesbians . . . it was just a book about two women. It was the first book about me."

The portrayal of lesbian identity in *Patience and Sarah* encouraged Moe to begin creating a positive construction of herself as a lesbian woman. At the age of sixteen, Moe had found a virtual sponsoring institution in this novel, opening up a possibility of constructing a lesbian identity that had to do with love, adventure, loyalty, and partnership—qualities that the heterosexist discourse with which Moe was familiar did not associate with a performance of lesbian identity. The story Moe told on the Bureau reflects much of the above history:

> I'm Moe, I'm twenty, a junior. I grew up with a happy childhood, a twin sister, and two loving parents. I had a vague sense of conflict, friction regarding the ways my parents wanted me to dress and act. They didn't have strict definitions of femininity, but they had expectations of how girls are.
>
> About sixth or seventh grade, my classmates decided I was a lesbian. Funny, 'cause I hadn't yet. I got beaten and harassed; I was scared for my life. I wanted to live, but it seemed like it was my fault, that I was doing something horrible.
>
> When I was fifteen, I fell in love with my best friend. It wasn't that I was attracted to women; I just wasn't attracted to men. One day I told her, "Guess what? I've fallen in love." She guessed all these men, then all these women. Finally she asked, "Me?" But she married and moved away to Georgia rather than hang with high school.
>
> It's safe here [at the university]; I have friends. I can be open . . . I'm comfortable with myself. My parents are good

with it. My father said, "As long as it's a Jewish woman." My mom said, "I'm bisexual, so it doesn't matter I suppose."

Moe told me that her main goal in telling these stories was to "present gay people as human . . . and complicated," and her second goal was to be a "role model . . . who went through a lot but now I'm happy and proud of who I am" for those audience members who were not yet "out" to themselves. In this presentation, she was clearly playing several roles—educator, insider, outsider, role model, and survivor. These are also identities Moe performed for classroom writing assignments.

I received two papers from introductory psychology classes from Moe as well as four papers from a gay-themed writer's workshop, a workshop facilitated by myself and another woman who identified as a lesbian. In our interview, Moe reflected on the importance of having a gay-themed writing class. We discussed how in her first assignment, an open letter to the class, she asserted that classes for non-gay people needed to represent "queers as very human and similar to them." Moe wrote how she welcomed the opportunity to explore more complicated themes in our class, saying she was "tired of centering a . . . queer studies class on what straight people might think." Audience mattered to Moe, and she was acutely aware of the differing needs of an audience and how those needs sometimes conflicted with her own. Moe's imagined audience for the gay-themed class— the one she created a role for in her first assignment for the class— was an audience that understood some basic "outlaw truths," for example, "gay people are human and complicated." Moe wrote four pieces for this class, alternately positioning herself as a creative/autobiographical writer of personal narrative and a researcher exploring cultural artifacts and language in the gay community.

Much of Moe's writing for the gay-themed class was in the genre of personal narrative. Even the more formal research papers Moe submitted included personal narratives. However, many of these more formal papers also contained injunctions and lessons that bordered on the language of demand, something she did not use in her panel presentations. One such paper, about the symbols and signs used in the gay community, had a didactic message. Moe ended the paper about symbols and signs with this conclusion:

> We therefore see how emblems and other symbols help those who come out of the closet to both recognize others who share their identity and to proclaim their pride in their identity. We therefore must make sure that all young people are taught what these emblems mean so that no one who would potentially gain from them [would] not know what they mean. We must also keep in mind the history behind such representations because the meaning of such a representation might change drastically over time.

Here Moe took on the identity of "teacher" or pedagogue, telling her audience what to do. This is much like Vincente's command, "Don't make me into a hairdresser," an injunction I never heard him make in his panel presentations.

This didactic stance was absent from the essays composed solely of personal narrative. In one of the introductory psychology papers, Moe responded to an assignment that asked students for an "account of a life-changing experience." Moe began the essay by describing her great-grandfather, a "poor Jewish tailor" who fled Russia as a thirteen-year-old boy and immigrated to the United States. She told readers that within a few years, her great-grandfather's entire family was "swept off the earth by Hitler." This was an event that caused her great-grandfather to develop a "generalized paranoia which affected my grandmother deeply."

Next, Moe told about her grandmother, who during World War II "left home to become a welder for the war effort." Though her grandmother later married, Moe said that her grandmother was "ridiculed by her family for being interested in such a masculine career." What Moe most remembered about this grandmother, whom she described as having a "great amount of sentimental joy" about her life as a welder, was how this woman told her repeatedly "that I should do what makes me happy, even if people don't understand."

In these first two paragraphs, Moe positioned her family members as survivors of political and social oppression, and specifically in her grandmother's case as a gender nonconformist. These two character sketches, which detailed some of the life-changing experiences of her relatives, set up the rest of the essay, in which Moe explained two of her own life-changing experiences. The first of these aligned Moe's identity with that of two of her relatives—a survivor of political and social oppression. In the second experience, Moe constructed herself as a privileged person coming to a greater consciousness about the intersection of racism and poverty.

The first experience Moe described was when she was sixteen and realized she was a lesbian. Moe noted that until then, she thought "little of political justice or social equality." She revealed that it was her experience of becoming a target of violence in high school that enabled her to begin to understand political justice and social equality, though she wrote, "I feared for my life and was utterly alone."

In this passage, Moe constructed herself as a close parallel to her great-grandfather, the lone survivor of his family. In the next paragraph, Moe described how finding the gay community, "a beautiful community of human beings . . . with a unique history," helped her to see that "being gay meant so much more than fear." Unlike her great-grandfather, whom she described as suffering from paranoia brought on presumably by fear, Moe constructed herself as a person with a community, and "gay" as "beautiful."

The last part of Moe's essay detailed how she worked with small children at a refugee camp in Edinburgh, Scotland, and how the "concrete reality" of racism and hunger collided for her in the realization that very few of these displaced people were white. While she was there, one of the children she had befriended died of a curable lung disorder, and she wrote how she sang the "Mourner's Kaddish, the Jewish prayer over the dead," as the community of refugees expressed themselves in their own religions. Here Moe identified herself as a volunteer, a participant-observer at the refugee camp, Jewish, and a friend.

Her final paragraph detailed how, having spent her money on food for the children, she lived for a week with the homeless of London, who she noted were "mostly black," which deepened her new understanding of racism and hunger. The passage ended with her flying home and her father taking her to an expensive restaurant in New York City with friends of his who showed Moe photos from a trip they had just taken. Moe concluded with these observations and reflections:

> There were many fancy people in the pictures. They were all white. I glanced at the menu. A meal costs $24. I remember overhearing the head of the children's program saying on the phone that my little friend's condition could have been cured with a single injection at birth, costing $18. Nausea welled up inside my stomach as the reality of racism and poverty came into my understanding. And so it goes: My cultural baggage.

Moe's final rhetorical construction of herself was of a privileged "self" coming to critical consciousness, weighted down by that privilege. The essay, like the Bureau story, used narrative to communicate the injustice of anti-Semitism, sexism, heterosexism, racism, and classism. We can see her performing the identity of "role model" as she did on the Bureau, offering encouragement to those who are punished for their religion, gender nonconformity, sexuality, and race. She also offered a mirror for those who are privileged by the discourses of racism and classism, though she stopped short of offering her audience a way to effectively intervene in these discourses.

Moe began writing as Moe Pontiack to the newspapers in her hometown when the gay youth group co-leader asked her to write about what it was like living as a closeted lesbian in high school. In response, Moe said, "I wrote to the papers many times . . . when I was in high school, saying . . . I'm a lesbian, this is my life."

Moe didn't stop with newspapers. Using her pseudonym, she wrote a letter to her principal describing "what kids are going through in high school": the abuse, the name calling. She told me that not long after she delivered the letter, she attended a Safe Schools meeting where she heard the principal describe the letter Moe had sent. Moe told me how the principal explained "how she got this letter a few weeks ago and she started crying when she read it, that it meant so much to her."

After hearing the principal's genuine concern and sadness, Moe gathered her courage and approached her, introducing herself as the

author of the letter. "She started crying and hugging me and everything. I could not believe it. It was the first time that something that
what I had . . . written . . . meant something. It wasn't just . . . me
needing to express myself."

This turning point enabled Moe to identify herself as an agent
for change, a writer who could move a real audience, no longer a writer
who used writing only as a safety valve for personal purposes of self-
expression. Since that moment, Moe told me, she had been "fasci-
nated with writing because . . . anyone can pick it up and read it. [It's]
like doing a speaker's bureau . . . but it reaches a lot more people."

Moe continued to use writing, creating for herself a social activist identity through the written word. Publicly occupying an "out"
lesbian identity was possible for Moe because she was able to do so
anonymously, to write anonymously. The sponsoring institution—
the youth support group that encouraged her to write anonymously—
was also a factor in Moe's rhetorical construction of herself as a positive, out, activist lesbian woman.

Moe's journal, like Vincente's, was another important audience/
sponsor. Before Moe found the youth support group, she identified
how putting her feelings in writing in her journal was an important
step, one she took before she told anyone about her feelings. Moe
discussed this moment in her interview with me:

> I said [wrote in her journal], "I'm in love with Jennifer." And
> then I erased it. Then I wrote it over again, and then the
> page—I still have it—it is like ripped, 'cause I erased it and
> said, like, "I can't imagine kissing her." Then I crossed it out
> and then wrote over it. I still have that journal entry, 'cause
> you know, it's the first time.

Indeed, this was the "first time" Moe constructed and performed a
rhetorical lesbian identity with the words "I'm in love with Jennifer.
. . . I can't imagine kissing her." Up until then, Moe told me, she had
constructed herself as carefree and happy in her journal:

> I was horribly—like, I was coming out and I was in agony
> over coming out. My guilt, you know, feelings people have.

> But I never wrote about them. I wrote, like, "I'm having a
> wonderful day. This is a beautiful day," and whatever, 'cause
> I wanted it to be true.

Moe felt as if she was "writing to a professor or . . . to my grandmother" in her journal, an audience whom she could not imagine
as an ally. In the interview with me, Moe talked about "lying" in her
diary and noted how she had since learned that "some psychologist
said if you're lying in your diary, you have pretty severe psychological problems. Or you're very troubled. I wasn't telling the truth at
all. The whole thing was a lie."

Moe was troubled by the way her peers used her gender nonconformity to create a stigmatized identity for her and also by her
own internalization of this stigmatized identity. She revealed the
extent of the trouble she was in to me not in our interview but instead in a four-page coming out story entitled "Coming Out." Moe
composed and distributed "Coming Out" the last three days of her
senior year in high school. Moe told me that "Coming Out" began
as a diary entry

> so I wouldn't forget it. I was afraid of forgetting it, 'cause I
> realized I was coming out to people in bad ways, in ways I
> didn't want to—like, in either anger or not knowing how
> to answer questions. And so I figured if I wrote it down and
> thought about it for a few days, I could just give them a piece
> of paper. I'd be, like, "Here, read it. This is my story." That
> came in real handy. I've given it to a lot of people.

Self-publishing and selectively distributing her own coming out
story under her given name, not a pseudonym, apparently enabled
Moe to create and claim a satisfying public rhetorical construction
of herself as a lesbian woman. Despite the importance of this moment, Moe told me she never mentioned writing or distributing
"Coming Out." When I asked her why, Moe told me it was because
the coming out story was based on a dream she had had about death.

Moe provided me with a copy of "Coming Out," interestingly
without her name on it. As I read it, I was reminded of Vincente's

exam essay. Like Vincente's apparent audience in the exam, Moe's audience for "Coming Out" had a need to understand in depth, with all the messy details, her coming out process. In "Coming Out," Moe described first how as even a "very small child" she had had a sense that she was somehow different from her friends. Moe identified this difference as revolving around her repeated insistence that she emphatically did not like a particular boy. She wrote that her friends "would often wonder why I insisted so strongly"; despite this, she said she could not tell them. She wrote: "I wanted them to know the truth, but they could not understand my truth because I could not find words to express it."

The next section detailed the first of many anxiety attacks that began in junior high.

> It was only years later that I realized that day would be the start of my coming out process. . . . I think that day I began to be reborn into an adult, and began to grow the strength to have an identity which was different and even hated by those around me.

The process of gathering the strength to claim/perform a lesbian identity first privately and later publicly lasted two years, and during this time Moe wrote that anxiety attacks were her "constant companion." She said that her fear was so intense that she could hardly eat and became very thin. Moe spoke of the last of these anxiety attacks as her "darkest memory," noting this time as another important turning point: "Everyone can look back over their life, and remember the point at which they had reached the single, sharp point that most fiercely tries their will to continue." It was following this anxiety attack that Moe had the dream about death, a dream "more real than life":

> I dreamed I was lying beside a familiar road. I saw the angel of death gliding past me. I wasn't afraid. I wasn't glad. I was just so very tired that him being there didn't matter. When he was about ten feet in front of me, he slowly held out a string in his ancient bony hand. It was made of a thread

that was brightly colored in an intricate design. I knew that
the thread was my life line. He held it up for me to see. It
was trailing to the floor and off into the distance. It was then
I knew my life could not end here. . . . I slowly . . . started
to drag myself down the sidewalk, past the ghost and down
the road. After a while I remember having the energy to
smile to myself because I knew then that I was now on my
feet, I could never be knocked down again.

Moe wrote she had little memory of the year following the dream
except "a slow, aching feeling that I was gay." In this narrative, Moe
moved from constructing herself as a victim to constructing herself
as a survivor and then as gay. Moe ended "Coming Out" with the
story of how she found a lesbian community. It was after this year
that she "met some gay people," and it was one of these new friends
who took Moe to her first "lesbian gathering." Moe was moved by
what she saw:

Hundreds of people who I knew were able to accept me, and
who knew the war I had fought with myself. The woman
who brought me saw my face. . . . She said, "Look around.
These are all your sisters." A powerful feeling came over me.
I had searched long and hard in a solitary journey, and after all this time, I had finally come home.

I was struck by the role writing had played in Moe's coming out
process. Using writing, Moe reconstructed herself from a victim of
heterosexist discourse and the physical assaults driven by that discourse to an active agent. As an agent, Moe constructed not only a
positive out lesbian identity but also an activist and educator identity.
It is clear from the case studies that students who were explicitly conscious of specific identity performance were much more likely
to make transfers across contexts and demonstrate success in these
other contexts. It is important to provide students with frames (varied genres, assignments, and classes that include alternative literacies—visual, theatrical, artistic) that help them become aware of the

ways in which they construct themselves rhetorically. This seems particularly important for students who, like the student speakers, need a frame and sponsoring institution that create a space for them to construct an ethos counter to the dominant, often stigmatizing, roles created for them by the dominant social discourses of heterosexism, sexism, racism, and so on.

In the concluding chapters, I explore how we might teach writing from an identity perspective so that it leads to rhetorical development instead of to "confessional" writing. I explore how we might use our understanding of specific identity performance, the Bureau as a sponsoring institution, and student speakers' experiences to create classrooms where all students can learn better how to negotiate academic and other discourses. I will examine classroom strategies and assignments that may assist students in using language to claim a positive identity for themselves and to thrive in the academy as well as to contribute to their own communities.

# 4 / Sponsoring Identity Negotiation in the Writing Classroom and Beyond

> Instead of writing herself away from the world, the course
> allowed her to write her way into it.
> —Karen Skolfield

**W**e have seen how the Speaker's Bureau fosters student speakers' ability to speak and write their way into the world of public discourse, to act as citizens contributing to the communities of which they are a part. In the quote above, my colleague Karen Skolfield describes how using identity-based writing enabled a particular student to write her most important personal concerns into the world of public issues in the gay, lesbian, and bisexual–themed writing course we designed and taught (a situation one step removed from the Bureau). Many in composition studies are wary of teaching writing from a personal, identity perspective, fearing students will write nothing more than confessional pieces and fail to develop the rhetorical tools necessary to thrive in the academy. I contend that teaching a guided examination of identity construction, identity politics, and the rhetorical work of specific identity performance can and does facilitate rhetorical growth in students in the mainstream writing classroom.

My aim is to help students in my writing classrooms to negotiate their multiple identities and create agency in shaping rhetorical situations, including addressing social justice issues in their communities and classrooms. This chapter is a blueprint, my own praxis—an example of how we might teach identity-based writing so that students see themselves as writers, speakers, mentors, and citizens who are able to consciously and specifically communicate their needs and values with humility and compassion. In this chapter, I outline how to create opportunities in the classroom that support students as they work to claim a positive sense of self, capable of using language as power *with* rather than *over* others, so that they can thrive in the academy and contribute to their own communities as well as to the world community.

What I introduce in this chapter highlights the importance of assisting students in seeing how they are both agents in discourse, able to create and perform identities for their own aims and for the benefit of their communities, as well as subjects, determined and shaped and always within those discourses. I emphasize the necessity of assisting students in identifying the "truths" that normative and alternative discourses purport so that students may decide—may consciously choose—which "truths" they want to reproduce, resist, or transform. I am convinced that the best way I can teach these valuable choices is to invite students to story their lived experiences and guide them to create specific identity performances. I have seen how doing so assists students in connecting the issues in their stories to the public conversation about those issues. Further, I believe it is imperative to offer students a way to address the real and enduring identity-based differences between themselves and their audiences. Doing so can enable students to create authority with their audiences and make allies of real audiences both inside and outside the classroom.

In this chapter, I discuss the ways we as writing teachers might do this work, particularly focusing on the three elements of sponsorship. I begin by reviewing how the Bureau functions as a sponsoring institution and detailing how we might adapt these elements of sponsorship for the writing classroom. I reflect second on how these elements of sponsorship were present in a gay, lesbian, and bisexual–themed writing course I taught some time ago. Last, I examine the presence of these elements of sponsorship in the general writing classroom and reflect on how we as teachers of general writing might better use these elements in the required writing classroom.

## Adapting Elements of the Speaker's Bureau

It is clear that student speakers' experience of crafting identities through the Bureau has a broader effect on their general writing and speaking. In particular, their work on the Bureau assists them in be-

coming more able and aware writers in the classroom. We can adapt
the uncommon elements of the Bureau to our own composition classrooms and assist our own students in negotiating identity amid competing social discourses and in becoming more able rhetoricians.

In the previous chapters, we have seen how the Speaker's Bureau
supports and guides student speakers to fashion and create specific
identity performances to achieve their aims. Student speakers do so
by learning to define and redefine their multiple and shifting identities and identity-based values. In the process, student speakers position themselves as educators. They also learn to offer roles for their
audiences, positioning audience members as allies willing to work
with them to transform heterosexism. The Bureau, functioning as a
sponsoring institution—a place where student speakers can learn to
use their stories for social action—provides this sponsorship to student speakers in three ways:

- The Bureau provides a unique forum that positions student speakers as educators and experts. The format of Bureau presentations allows student speakers to enter classrooms as invited guest speakers and to set and guide the
  agenda, including introducing and negotiating ground rules
  with the audience.
- The Bureau provides student speakers with a lens through
  which to see the "truths" that heterosexist discourse purports and the "truths" that counter- or outlaw discourses
  assert. Student speakers in turn offer this lens to audiences
  so that they too can see alternative, outlaw "truths" and heterosexist "truths" about those people who claim an identity of or who are identified as GLBT.
- The Bureau provides student speakers with strategies, guiding speakers to "get specific," to use their lived experiences
  to create specific identity performances.

The ethos that "getting specific" calls for is one that rests on
identifying and addressing differences in identity-based values. These
strategies assist student speakers in acknowledging identity-based
value differences between themselves and their intended audiences
and help them select and story their lived experiences accordingly.

Students then learn to perform alternately as insiders and outsiders relative to the positions that normative social discourses offer. Performing specific identities through these stories gives student speakers a way to build and perform an ethos based in specificity and in turn to create identification between themselves and their audiences. In the process, student speakers introduce and reference "truths" about "gay people" from competing discourses, inviting audience members to examine multiple truths about what it might mean to live as a gay, lesbian, bisexual, or transgendered person.

It is in this way that student speakers focus on *creating* allies who claim very different identities rather than on *finding* allies who share a sameness of identity. The stories student speakers tell in Bureau presentations invite audiences into the position of becoming allies in the struggle to create a just community for all people.

The student speakers in the case studies also drew on these three elements of sponsorship in their writing. In particular, I noted how student speakers responded to school writing assignments and written exams by positioning themselves in more authoritative roles, by "getting specific" as they storied their lived experiences and communicated conflicting "truths," and by constructing and performing specific identities through those stories to persuade their audiences to become allies and to work with them on particular issues.

Student speakers have a "real" situation and a compelling exigency with which to cope: a campus climate shaped to a large degree by homophobic discourse and the emotional, social, and physical dangers that are the material consequences of homophobic discourse. The goal of these student speakers is to create a counter-, outlaw discourse that celebrates GLBT expressions and champions civil rights for all. The material consequences they hope will follow are an environment of safety and justice for all. Students in our required composition classrooms typically are not aware of "real" situations and exigencies that do indeed shape their own experiences, unless they are familiar with being marginalized. As teachers of writing, our job is as much about developing this awareness in students as it is about inviting students to see their own intersectionality/multiple identities. This can create what Joseph Petraglia calls pseudotransactionality, setting up situations in the classroom that provide students with the sense of urgency associated with "live" writing meant to "do something" in the world outside of the classroom. It is not easy to set up the sort of rhetorical situations in the classroom that the Bureau assists student speakers in identifying and addressing. The next section and the classroom suggestions that follow address this conundrum.

### The Writing Classroom Is Not a Bureau Presentation Site

It's important to revisit and consider the complexities that arise when we try to envision how to create a site in a writing classroom like that of the Speaker's Bureau presentation site. The differences between speaking to classes as a guest from the Speaker's Bureau and participating as a member of that class are distinct; the writing classroom is not a Bureau presentation site. The students in our classrooms do not expect to be speakers, to set and control the agenda—they expect to be the audience for a teacher who does so and who is positioned as the educator and expert. The curriculum of a writing course differs in significant ways from the curriculum that guides Bureau training workshops. This is true both of the themed writing classroom and the required writing classroom. The common elements between the Bureau and many (but not all) writing classrooms include an invitation to connect personal concerns to the public realm through language, guidance in understanding composing as a series of choices, and instruction in fashioning an ethos to move audiences. In addition, the Bureau curriculum guides student speakers to

- perform specific identities amongst competing social discourses,
- identify "truths" embedded in these social discourses,
- attend to differences in identity-based values between themselves and their audiences,
- and make allies by attending to these differences in identity-based values in order to locate and offer strategies that might work for all the parties involved.

The goal of a writing course that provides this sort of sponsorship, as I envision it, is shaped by my particular slant on ethos: the conscious creation of specific identity performances in order to position audience members as allies and move them to action. In order to do so, we as writing teachers need to do the following:

- Offer students in our classrooms positions or roles that are valued as well as active as opposed to passive.
- Invite students to see themselves as agents in and subjects of multiple and competing discourses and to identify the "truths" those discourses purport.
- Guide students to address the important and enduring differences in identity-based values between themselves and their audiences.
- Invite students to use writing and speaking to position themselves as allies with their audiences and position their audiences as potential allies.

I propose that we teach students that they can invite audiences to become allies around issues important to them and move those people to action. We can teach students to "get specific" and draw on their lived experiences and choose how they construct and perform a variety of specific identities to persuade audiences. We can create opportunities for students to see how their agency or autonomy is necessarily bounded by the discourses, the cultural norms and "truths," that define their concepts of the world, one another, and themselves. The main goal, then, is to teach students to think critically about identity construction and performance and ground that understanding in specificity. Doing so will encourage students to analyze and deconstruct cultural claims, norms, and "truths" as texts and in turn to analyze and deconstruct claims in any kind of text—including academic arguments. In the process, we can show students how to connect their personal needs—for acceptance, contribution, integrity—to the public realm. I turn my attention first to the themed writing classroom to consider how the three elements of sponsorship might function in this sort of class.

## One Step Removed from the Bureau: The GLBT-Themed Writing Course

Karen Skolfield and I used Harriet Malinowitz's book, *Textual Orientations: Lesbian and Gay Students and the Making of Discourse Com-*

*munities,* to create the basic curriculum of the class, which was called Needing to Shout! Gay, Lesbian, and Bisexual Voices. This class was an experimental writer's workshop I team-taught with Karen some years ago. While this class was not part of the ethnographic study upon which this book is based, I believe it will be instructive to look at how the contexts of themed writing classrooms are and are not like a Bureau presentation site.

In a conference paper, Karen eloquently explained the questions both she and I had grappled with as teachers in the required writing classroom; these questions prompted us to propose this GLBT-themed writing workshop:

> How can I encourage my gay students to get past the explanations and write in a way that validates rather than defends their lives? Part of a composition course is learning to tailor writing to an audience—fine in most cases but not when the audience is potentially hostile or, at best, uninformed. How can students focus their writing energy on themselves and their deeper interests instead of on background for a presumed heterosexual audience? (1–2)

These were the questions that guided us, questions consonant with the concerns Malinowitz raises in her book about the importance of themed classrooms for GLBT students.

Like Bureau workshops and presentations, Needing to Shout! was a place where we examined the "truths" purported by normative discourses and contrasted them with outlaw or non-normative "truths." Though we did not talk in terms of discourses, specificity, or the performance of identity, nonetheless these poststructural ideas existed, just as they exist on the Bureau. And in fact, we read and discussed two chapters from Shane Phelan's book *Getting Specific,* chapters where Phelan used her personal experience to articulate her theory of specificity. We did "do" identity performance and subversive repetition—though it went unnamed—and we noted together who used what words and for what purposes, implicitly delineating the discourse of homophobia and heterosexism and working together to articulate an outlaw discourse with its own "truths."

The assignments we devised invited students to use their lived experiences to compose creative writing as well as analytic writing. Students wrote in response to analytic readings, poems, short stories, and films. We were intent on offering students opportunities to hear their own voices, to perform a variety of identities in a variety of genres, in response to authors and directors who identified not only as GLBT but also as black, Latino, Asian, Jewish, working class, and other less charged social affiliations. We hoped that by doing so, students would be able to consider experientially how intersectionality worked in their own lives and in the lives of the authors and characters we encountered.

Like the student speakers on the Bureau, students in Needing to Shout! were a self-selected group interested in these "voices." Students were invited to draw on their own lived experiences and connect those experiences to the class texts as we explored coming out narratives, the meaning of family, survival strategies, and projects defined by the students' own individual interests. Three of the five focal student speakers who appear in this book—Moe, Sulli, and Jamar—enrolled in this class while they were participating in the ethnographic study this book is based upon.

This themed class functioned as a sponsoring institution in a number of ways. The class structure positioned students as writers, experts, and educators and asked students to take power—with us as teachers and with the writers and directors we introduced—and to discuss on paper and with one another the ideas presented in the course material as well as ideas based on their own lived experiences. We also utilized peer review and the publication and presentation of students' work, affording students an audience of their peers and instructors and the positions of academic reviewer and co-editor. Though the students in a themed writing class do not enjoy the anonymity or authority that a student speaker on the Bureau enjoys as a guest speaker, students felt at liberty to name the important issues in their lives and trusted they could pursue these issues with safety in this class. In fact, students raised the question of why we had not included transgendered voices from the beginning, a question we addressed later in the class by providing pieces by transgendered authors.

The structure of the class differed from the usual positioning of students as passive and compliant: the class was pass/fail, students chose the class as an elective, and students were invited to introduce and explore topics of interest to them. Evaluation consisted of detailed feedback from peers and instructors meant to coach students as fellow writers aiming to communicate clearly and passionately. Although the students in our class were graded on their performances, they had much more room to negotiate and influence the impact of grading on their thinking and writing. By contrast, student speakers perform outside of this economy, and though they solicit and read audience evaluations, they do so for the most part in light of their own aims.

The class, then, like the Bureau, did offer students expert and educator roles as well as passive student roles. As students enrolled in a class, they did not expect to introduce topics or set the agenda. Because the class was a writer's workshop, they were positioned as writers, and because the content of the class invited students to use their own lived experiences as valid texts—as valid as any of the texts chosen by myself and Karen—students were to a degree positioned as experts and educators. The assignments themselves assisted students in seeing their own intersectionality and in claiming and speaking from these multiple, in-process identities.

Some students had already taken up the position of educators or activists before they enrolled in the class, and some had not. A few saw themselves as writers; most identified as GLBT and assumed others in class shared their identities. In the first assignment, an open letter published in class and addressed to the entire class, students and instructors alike explained what brought them to the class and what they hoped to learn. These letters immediately addressed how students felt positioned as outsiders by homophobic and heterosexist discourses and their wish to take agency and resist these discourses.

Sulli noted in his open letter how he felt positioned as an outsider in his college writing class (the first-year required course at the university) and how he imagined he would feel as an insider in this class:

I had hoped college writing would help me with my need to relay my thoughts on paper. I found, unfortunately, that the setting of my college writing course was far too reminiscent of high school. . . . When I saw my chance to go to this class, I jumped at it. I figured there was no way that I would feel uncomfortable in this setting.

Clara Stone positioned herself in similar ways, exercising her poetic voice in her own open letter:

Open is how I'd love to be. . . . I'm hesitating to spare the response. I can't stand straightness sometimes, I withhold the freak until it's slipping out. . . . I get tired, I get used, I crave to be craved, I vent on this paper and to [your] receiving ears, my heart skips when I hear of companions. You remind me and empower me in my struggles that I am not alone. . . . I thank this class for existing, suppression has had its turn.

Both these students spoke to the ways they had been positioned by others, by the discourse of heterosexism. David Sandburg, then a twenty-three-year-old graduating senior, spoke most directly to the importance of this themed writing class in relation to the effects of internalized heterosexism on his life in his own open letter:

I enrolled in this writing class because I thought it would give me an opportunity to discuss and write about GLBT issues in an open safe environment.

I have been out of the closet now for about a year. Coming out was one of the most difficult experiences of my life. It took up an entire semester of my life. There were weeks I could not eat, sleep, or even focus on one thing.

More than anything, students spoke to their need for a place to be honest and safe. Moe told me in her interview that it was a relief for her to stop imagining her audience as straight people who understood nothing about what it means to live as a lesbian, a gay man, or a bisexual. Moe relished the idea that she didn't have to explain *why* she was lesbian and instead could drop into a consideration of particular issues with which she grappled on a day-to-day basis. In her open letter, Moe reflected on the role she would have liked to see straight allies play as members of this themed writing class, explicitly positioning her classmates as allies.

> Straight allies should be encouraged to come [join the class], but I end up feeling that they must be allies. They cannot come into the class with the attitude, "Okay, tell me one good reason why I should not hate you."

Moe went on to describe a range of identities she saw GLBT people occupying, emphasizing again the importance of having a place where it is unnecessary to spend time convincing anyone that

> gay people are not some sick alien race. . . . There are all sorts of gay people: white, black, handicapped, artistic, cruel, helpless romantics, elderly, pessimistic, etc., I am tired of centering a class made for queer studies on what straight people might think.

Note that Moe's response in particular shows an awareness of the limitations of heteronormative discourses even in a class on queer studies. Moe took this class during the third year she was a student speaker on the Bureau, and I believe this is part of what enabled her to articulate so clearly her take on heteronormative discourses as well as intersectionality.

In these letters, it is clear that the students saw themselves as oppressed by the discourses they had encountered and were actively seeking to assert their agency, their "voices," to protest the way heterosexist discourse had positioned them. The open letters illuminated students' personal needs and their hopes as well as the identities they claimed and those stigmatized identities others had given them. All felt hopeful that the goals of the class would assist them in meeting needs for safety, respect, and understanding and would be a challenge as well. Similarly, some students joined the Speaker's

Bureau because they assessed that their own goals were reflected by those of the Bureau.

In the second assignment, students analyzed patterns in coming out narratives, in the process defining and redefining the "truth" about coming out. In his paper, Sulli talked about coming out as breaking isolation and then contemplated what it might mean to come out in the vastly different gay communities that exist. He went on to question what it means to "become" gay, asking, "What are they becoming?" In the end, Sulli argued for a concept of coming out linked more to political beliefs than to sexual behavior or identity. What I noticed about Sulli's interpretations was how grounded they were in the "queer"-identified New York City scene from which he had just come. Sulli understood the concept of "queer" as a coalition-based political *stance* where people who identified in many different ways actively worked together against heteronormative "truths" rather than as an *identity* or behavior where people organized around sameness of identity (identity politics) to combat oppressive "truths."

In the process of defining coming out, many students defined the space of the closet and the "truths" of heterosexism that necessitated the creation of that closet. Delia Bouchard explained this necessity in her own paper, exploring the ramifications of internalizing the "truths" of heterosexism:

> We built the closet because we were afraid, and we stayed in it because, in too many ways, we were right to be afraid. . . . One of the greatest weapons heteronormative society has to combat the alarming spread of open homosexuality: our own fears and self hatred. That is why this can so often be the most trying part of coming out—how can you convince someone else you are not deranged or diseased if you cannot convince yourself?

The GLBT-themed writing classroom was a safe space to explore that question for Delia and the others, to admit that they too struggled with internalized heterosexism. The class was a place where students could take a rest from the task of making allies and look at the obstacles that made it difficult to make allies, such as the heterosexist "truths" they too had internalized. It was also a place to begin again to strategize just how to make allies.

The strategies we used to explore these conflicting "truths" were grounded in specificity, in getting specific about the multiple and in-process identities and identity-based values we each performed—though again, while we did not use that language, we did reference Phelan's work. We asked students to begin, as Phelan did in the selections we read, with the details of their own lives and to note the differing positions they occupied as women and men of different racial/cultural and class backgrounds. Both Sulli and Delia used stories from their own lives to complicate the "truth" of what it means to come out and to contest both mainstream beliefs as well as the theories and examples emerging from the GLBT-identified writers and directors we studied.

Moe conducted research for her final project about the use of words by and for those identified as queer, gay, lesbian, bisexual, and transgendered. The paper emerged from discussions and even arguments the class members had about using the word "queer" and about what it meant and to whom. We discussed our differences in identity-based values: generational differences (students hated *Desert Hearts,* a film Karen and I loved) and differences around race and ethnicity and class and how those identifiers influenced our values and the way we understood each other and words we chose to use.

Ian Smith in particular questioned the "truths" he believed the gay community asserts about coming out and what it means to be gay, grounding his assertions in his own specific identity performance:

> This is the problem I had with the coming-out narratives we have read: that they did not accurately describe the coming-out experiences of me and many other gay people. There are many of us out here who feel excluded by the straight community for our sexuality, but equally ignored by the gay "community" for not following the traditional patterns of behavior which have been "prescribed" for homosexuals. . . . The type of coming-out narrative which I have always pre-

ferred [is] one that deals with homosexuality as simply who
you sleep with and who you are attracted to, rather than as
a part of one's culture.

Notice that the students in this class performed a range of "gay" identities, from Sulli's concept of politically based "queer" to Ian's behav-
iorally based "gay." There was room in the class for both "truths" to
exist simultaneously and, further, room for disagreement and deliberation on what each "truth" might mean to the varied "gay" communities and the other communities to which we all belonged.

Ian continued to explore his dissatisfaction with what he saw
as the "prescribed" behavior for "homosexuals" in the gay community in his final project. Again, Ian drew on his own experiences, noting his own confusion as he attempted to identify with what was
visibly the gay male community. In particular, Ian described in his
final paper how he could not subscribe to the "gay community's . . .
approaches to ideal beauty—enshrining the boyish appeal of the
young smooth-skinned, gym-toned dumb blonde surfer." Instead,
Ian introduced the class to the "Bear Community," a group of gay men
who, according to Ian, are

all genuine men being themselves . . . having overcome the
self-limiting belief that we had to conform to media images
of gay male beauty, images that either we did not fit, and
never would, or which were of no sexual interest to us.

Ian's ideas prompted discussions in class about how the "Bear
Community" seemed to be a response to lookism or sexism, not
unlike the responses that many feminist and lesbian feminist communities have to the mass media portrayal of ideal feminine beauty.
Inherently we were questioning the "truths" of beauty, how the media
used those "truths" to manipulate us, and how those "truths" fed into
oppression via sexism and racism in particular.

Many students used fiction, creating characters who occupied
a variety of specific identities simultaneously to explore issues of importance to them. Catherine Long chose to create such a character,

one who complicated what it means to claim a bisexual identity. Catherine sketched Ellie, the main character, as a serious student, conscientious in her relationships. In Catherine's introduction, she wrote about the importance of monogamy in relation to claiming a bisexual identity, questioning what is "true" about those who live as bisexual people.

> I wrote this story which focuses on the question of monogamy. . . . This question goes beyond me personally. . . . When a bisexual person comes out, they are often assumed to be unable to be monogamous because they have the capability of dating a member of either sex. For myself, I feel I am a monogamous person.

Whether creative or expository, these writings reflected a group of students seriously engaged in critically examining the conflicting "truths" of what it might mean to claim a GLBT identity complicated by race and class and other identity markers. The space of the themed writing classroom provided some common ground; it allowed students to address particular issues and invite their classmates to become allies, to understand, for example, that the ideal of gay male beauty can be limiting for some, as can the notion that bisexual people are necessarily non-monogamous. In these pieces, I saw students writing about what mattered personally to them and connecting those issues to the world of public discourse.

Who comes together for what purpose and under what terms clearly distinguishes the themed writing classroom space from that of a general writing classroom and, further, from a speaker's bureau presentation site. Despite these real and apparent differences, I have found that students in both the themed and the general writing classroom can and do benefit from Bureau-like opportunities and sponsorship in the writing classroom.

*Identity Talk in the Required Writing Classroom*
I developed the curriculum I use in the required writing courses I've taught from the training I received at the California State University at Chico (CSUC) and the University of Massachusetts at Am-

herst (UMass at Amherst). This training was based in teaching writing as a process in a workshop structure. In this section, I focus on the college writing classes I taught from 2000 to 2004, first at UMass at Amherst and then at Franklin Pierce College (FPC is a small liberal arts college in New Hampshire). Like the class Needing to Shout!, these classes were not part of the ethnographic study upon which this book is based, and though I was unable to flag these courses as having a theme when students registered, I did create a theme for the college writing classes I taught, a theme guided by the theory of specific identity performance.

Instead of focusing on a specific set of identities as a theme, like GLBT identities, I focused on the broad theme of identity, allowing students to explore their multiple and shifting identities, both those that make them feel "different" and those that confer privilege. In response, students focused on the usual race, class, and gender or explored identities based on culture, degree of ability, age, or physical stigmas or even identities such as athlete, artist, or musician. I subtitled these required writing courses "Writing That Matters" and focused assignments on identity and representation. The assignments, in order, asked students to write about and decide how to represent

- themselves as writers in a personal essay,
- a way in which they were stereotyped by others and their responses to that stereotype in an open letter to a younger person,
- a fictional conversation with published authors on ideas in those authors' published works in a piece that documented the conversation either in the format of a standard academic essay or as a talk show or correspondence,
- an issue important to a community to which they belonged in a personal research essay,
- their reflections on the writing and reviewing they had done over the course of the semester in a reflective essay or letter (see appendix A for each of these assignments as they were distributed to students).

Identity as a focus opened up a space for students to look at the ways they had positioned themselves and others as well as at the ways others had positioned them in relation to their identities, both privileged and not so privileged. This invited students to become conscious of and examine the lens, the identity-based values, they were using to make sense of the world and themselves. The assignments asked students to use their lived experiences as texts and to begin to explore how the lenses they used were shaped by dominant as well as outlaw or counter-normative discourses. I guided students to connect the discourses germane to their identities and the issues important to them and helped them begin to formulate how they might connect first with an audience that shared some identity important to students and then with audiences that did not share any of those identities.

I began this work by creating a sponsoring institution in the required writing classroom, one that fostered the conscious creation of specific identity performances, by

- offering students positions or roles that are valued and active as opposed to passive,
- inviting students to see themselves both as agents in and subjects of multiple and competing discourses and to identify the "truths" those discourses purport,
- guiding students to address the important and enduring differences in identity-based values between themselves and their audiences,
- and inviting students to use writing to position themselves as allies with their audiences and position their audiences as potential allies.

### Students, Writers, Mentors, and Citizens: Offering Students Choices

Attending to how students have been positioned as writers and students when they enter our classrooms and reflecting on the positions we want to offer students in our writing classrooms is important. As I noted at the beginning of chapter 2, most students use words like "slow" or "boring" to describe themselves as writers at the start of the semester. When I ask where they get this image of themselves as writers, students cite numerous comments—marginalia—on previous school essays from their teachers that position them in these ways. And in fact, very few see themselves as "writers" at all.

The students in our required writing courses do not come to class as writers or as a self-selected affinity group, and many do not come with their own goals in mind. Required writing courses are typically made up of students who are fulfilling a requirement and simply happen to be in our particular classroom because it fits their schedules. Our educational institutions position first-year students (passive recipients of knowledge) as non-writers or at least as unfamiliar with college writing standards and thus in need of a required writing class (mediation for deficits located in the students). As a result, many students align themselves with this position or resist this positioning and position themselves as resentful victims of an unnecessary requirement.

In addition, the students in our classes are unable to choose their audience; most have not consciously considered who their classmates or instructor might be as an audience. The students do not have the sort of common ground with one another that student speakers or those who choose a themed course do. Our students do not enjoy the anonymity or authority of a guest speaker nor the camaraderie those in the GLBT-themed course expect to find. We cannot exactly replicate this guest speaker collaborative or camaraderie experience in the required writing classroom, even if we theme the class, ask students to find a common issue, and have them collaborate with one another, using their own stories to construct a presentation or essay for the class. Students' need for autonomy and meaning is unlikely to be fully met in this scenario.

Finally, the students in our classes are graded on their performances. The goal of learning what the teacher wants and getting a good or at least passing grade for this required class is necessarily elevated over any personal goals students might have in the school's economy of grades linked to reward-punishment. On the other hand, student speakers and the students in the pass/fail GLBT class have more autonomy as neither is required, nor are grades an issue.

Much has been said about creating a forum that positions students in more authoritative roles in the required writing classroom. In particular, Robert Brooke's book, *Writing and Sense of Self: Iden-*

*tity Negotiation in Writing Workshops,* describes the importance of positioning students as writers by teaching writing as a workshop. Introducing the writing class as a writer's workshop where the intention is to work together as writers invites students to see themselves as workshop members and writers. Brooke notes that we can further this positioning by divorcing grades as much as possible from the writing process or product; we can use grading contracts instead that simply specify the amount of work to be done and the deadlines for this work as well as participation in class as the basis for grading (see appendix C for an example of a grading contract).

Less has been said about positioning students as mentors, citizens, and writers in a civic context. John Dewey spoke directly to the importance of teaching students to be citizens, and most recently Tom Deans, along with a number of other proponents of community service–learning, has thoroughly explored and examined the value of inviting students to link their private concerns with community issues in the public realm. I contend that doing so is another important way to position students in more authoritative roles.

Part of positioning students as writers and citizens in my writer's workshop is to ask students to reflect on many of their assignments and workshop experiences in process notes. I begin this practice on the first day of class. I ask students in the last ten minutes of that first day of writing and discussion to write me a "Dear Zan" letter:

> Please write me a note,
> "Dear Zan, this is what worked for me this class; this is what didn't." Also, tell me in your note:
> What do you want me to know about YOU as a writer, workshop participant, and a person?
> What do you want to know about ME as a writer, a workshop facilitator, and a person?
> I'll write you back.

Implicit in this assignment is an invitation to students to position themselves outside of the passive student role and to occupy more active roles, in particular the role of writer, a position valued in the academy. Asking students to think about three roles they play in the workshop and outside the workshop as well as about the roles I play outside and inside the classroom creates an opportunity to begin thinking about intersectionality, how we each occupy a variety of multiple identities simultaneously. In the notes I receive from students, I learn what they like to write about or what they prefer to do instead of write, and I hear about how comfortable or not they are regarding participating in the class as well as about things they enjoy about themselves—they like baseball, they know how to be a good friend, or they think of themselves as open-minded. They ask me what I like to write, where I get my ideas for class assignments, or if like teaching and want to know what my hobbies are; sometimes they ask me big questions like, "What event in your life has changed you the most?" or, "Why are you interested in social action?" Right away, we get to see each other as more than the usual adversaries of "teacher" and "student" and how we all have many facets. I enjoy writing back, simply affirming I've heard them, connecting where I can. I answer the questions seriously: I tell them I enjoy writing poetry, nonviolence informs my teaching, and I like to teach, garden, bike, do yoga, and cook; I tell them getting clean and sober has been the event that changed my life the most, and my activism in the gay civil rights movement makes social action very important to me.

In other process notes, I ask students to describe what they are learning as writers and what they hope each piece accomplishes. Again, this has become a common practice, one that I also learned through my training, particularly at UMass at Amherst. I respond to student reflections as a reader and as a fellow writer too, clearly describing in my comments on assignments what it is about the student's writing that meets my values as an academic reader and what doesn't and what might. In my response to Garrett Boyd's research/personal paper on gender roles in his dorm, I had this to say:

Dear Garrett,

When I read your paper I could see your experiences, what your world is like, and I was drawn into the piece. Your use of your own story, the survey results you collected, and the library sources you reference helped me to trust your credibility, your ethos. When you interpreted the quotes you used from your sources, I understood your logic (logos), while the story and the voice you used to guide me appealed to my emotions (pathos). Here are my questions:

- What do you think it means that men are more uncomfortable wearing "gender inappropriate" clothes?
- Is it necessary to get rid of roles or have a different relationship to them?
- I need a copy of your survey and more information in your works cited; see my notes.

Thanks, Zan

We can further that conversation by creating a dialogue: asking students to say back, describe, what they heard us saying in our evaluation and tell us what needs of theirs as writers were met or unmet in relation to our feedback, where they agree or disagree and why. Or, quite as useful, we can give this kind of feedback in face-to-face conferences. I often see the impact of this dialogue in notes to me, at conferences, and sometimes in the essays students submit. In Jim Taylor's case, he incorporated traces of our dialogue into his fictional conversation with two authors, creating a personal/academic essay hybrid that reflected his thinking. The assignment asked students to do a close reading of two published essays and connect the ideas in those essays to their own experiences. In the excerpt below, Jim tells readers how with feedback he was able to separate his own reactions to the essay from what the author, Eli Clare, was articulating and how in doing so he found unexpected common ground with the author.

> I read . . . "The Mountain" by Eli Clare. The only emotion I felt when I read this piece was anger. How dare this person give up! Upon reading that last line, my anger at her for writing such a piece bubbled over into my writing, and soon I had written a rather angry piece to her about how she had made me feel.
>
> At the urging of my professor, I reached within myself to find the true source of my anger. I found it in my past. . . .

I've been told by many people to keep climbing that meta-
phorical mountain. This struggle to be the best, no matter how unlikely, was a very strong part of my social identity. . . . After my talk with my professor, I came to the realization that Eli and I wanted the same thing: a chance to take
a break.

Jim's realization that what Clare was speaking to was a need for rest
and self-acceptance—which is not the same as giving up—led him
to think critically about his beliefs about himself and others and
where those beliefs originated. He followed the above paragraph with
his response to the other published author:

Bobbie Harro's piece on the cycle of socialization [states that]
what we are is dictated by where we are, who is around us,
and what they are saying. Normally I would've dismissed
this thinking out of hand; but after reading Clare's piece [I
thought] How can I possibly understand how things are, when
I don't understand who I am and what makes me think the
way I do?

This emphasis on dialogue, about writing and about ideas, furthers
students' sense of themselves as co-writers in a writer's workshop able
to respond to other writers, including those who are published.

Peer review is another important place where we as teachers of
writing can offer students the position of writer as well as editor. The
portfolio that students submit at the end of the semester includes
letters both to and from a peer writer about writing. In the excerpts
below, students take up the role of coach and editor as they assess
one another's writing over the course of the semester.

Dear Claudine,

I enjoyed reading Leap of Faith, you had a solid story . . . a
nice job describing the events. . . . If you added more details
the picture formed in my mind might have been a little more
clear. . . . Did other students put as much time and effort into

their piece as you? Maybe you could tie into why it was so important for you to do this. I didn't really notice many proofreading mistakes, and the tone and style of the paper does seem to acknowledge audience.

Sincerely,

Amber Jensen

Dear Amber,

After reading [the first paragraph of] "Is it Worth it to Hate?" I wanted to know what happened to you, I wanted to understand your passion for the subject. Your passion is then revealed in the great ethos you create, really pulling the reader to your side because of how you and your family are directly related to one side of the issue. . . . The few mistakes were in one large paragraph and a sentence that should have been in quotation marks (". . . To take away the sensitivity . . . . book without words").

Good Luck in School,

Claudine Abdul

This exchange shows how student have learned to become editors who can make specific, concrete observations about the essays their peers give them to read and can separate these observations from their evaluations and suggestions. Persistently offering students the role of peer reviewer enables students to learn to coach one another. I have had the most success with peer review by teaching it as an integral part of the class, as central as the writing itself: teaching peer review explicitly for each of the essay assignments; using peer review instead of instructor feedback on drafts for the first and third essays in a series of four multiple draft essays; and incorporating peer review as an essential component of the portfolio review process.

Offering students these more active roles is one way we can begin to create a composition classroom that is for and about writers and readers—a writer's workshop akin to a speaker's bureau—where writers work at saying what matters to them and fashioning roles for themselves as well as for an audience capable of responding.

*Identifying "Truths": Inviting Students to See Through*
*New Lenses*

As students take up new positions, we begin to look together at the "truths" in their own lived experiences and those in published essays as well as in the media. Above, Jim Taylor explicitly thought about the "truth" of what he has been told about how to live life by pushing himself to climb ever higher mountains. In the process of Jim's close reading of Clare and Harro and his examination of his own lived experiences, he created a new "truth" about living that included rest and self-acceptance as well as the idea that we are each shaped by what we are taught to believe.

First-year students in particular are in a position to understand the idea that what is "true" in one place or time or to one person is not necessarily "true" in another or to another. For example, what was "true" about diversity at home is often not "true" at school. White middle-class students from all-white towns think it is "true" that UMass at Amherst and FPC have much racial/ethnic diversity. The recruiting material often reflects this "truth" back to them. However, for students of color coming from communities of color, it is not "true" that these campuses are diverse—instead, what is "true" is that this is a mostly white community. The statistics in both institutions' records confirm the "truth" that students of color have noted—at the most, 20 percent of the student body is nonwhite at UMass at Amherst and FPC.

Often, first-year students are also acutely aware of their identity. As Moe and Vincente and many other student speakers noted in interviews and presentations, coming to a new school offers a person the opportunity to become somebody he or she could not be at home—most notably for GLBT students, the ability to construct a public GLBT identity.

Offering first-year students a lens to critically examine the ways normalizing social discourses and social institutions constrain their lives and the lives of others is crucial to students' ability to see differing "truths." Guiding students to identify the alternate or outlaw discourses they already know can open up new possibilities and choices regarding rhetorical identity construction. Linda Brodkey's experience with writing curriculum at Texas, where students looked at legal decisions on certain civil rights acts, had a similar aim. Others who are investigating the use of alternative discourses are Morris Young in Asian American discourse, Malea Powell and Scott Lyons in Native American discourse, and Lillian Bridwell-Bowles in feminist discourse. This lens, as I envision it, can assist us to teach a kind of critical thinking, important for self-reflection on identity construction and for analysis of claims in any kind of text, including academic arguments.

The lens I offer students is drawn directly from my slant on ethos, specific identity performance; I offer it primarily through experiential exercises where students begin to name the contingent nature of "truth" as well as the multiple social identities they perform and the relative importance of each identity.

In chapter 2, I noted how we might introduce the notion that we all position and perform our identities through language. We can use exercises that call deliberate attention to how we all position ourselves by inviting students to write and draw from the position of writer, noting the differing ways students represent themselves as writers or not. We can follow this exercise by asking students about the sort of remarks and comments they have received on their school writing assignments and list the judgments students report, noting aloud as we make the list how most of the judgments reference a deficit, a lack or void of talent on the part of the student, and give little description of what it is the evaluator is seeing or wanting. This time we can call attention to how students have been positioned by these judgments as "good" or "bad" students or writers, and we can note how many have internalized these judgments and act accordingly. It is from this frame that we can begin to speak to the relationship between the way we are positioned and the ways in which we position ourselves through language.

To further assist students in identifying the ways they have been positioned and position themselves as well as the idea of intersectionality, I use the "Dot Game," which I first learned from Matt Ouellette at the Center for Teaching at UMass at Amherst. The "Dot Game," or "What's on Top" as I call it, begins with assigning identities to different colored round "dot" stickers (see appendix A, essay 3, "Exploratory Draft Begun in Class"). For instance, I assign each colored sticker an identity such as:

blue = occupation
yellow = gender
green = race/ethnicity
red = other

Students are then asked to arrange the stickers on themselves in the order of importance of each identity to them. I ask students to consider which identity they are most aware of in the course of any day. Students share in small groups how they ordered these identities and then discuss what they noticed about the exercise and what their observations might mean.

As students report to the large group, I guide the discussion to highlight the point that often what we are least aware of is linked to how that identity is valued in the culture. For example, often white students note that race/ethnicity is low on their list. One student told me, "I know I'm not aware of my race/ethnicity because most places where I go, everyone is white like me." Another student noted, "Occupation's the most important thing for me now, the job of being a student. In computer science, my major, everyone's like me: a man and white, well, some are Asian. So I don't notice I'm a man or white." From this place, we can begin to talk about who might notice their race/ethnicity or gender and why, which leads us to think about cultural norms and beliefs and how those produce inequities.

We discuss what the mainstream media's role is in the creation and reproduction of norms and beliefs, what the media makes "true" about men and women, about gay, lesbian, bisexual, heterosexual, and transgendered people, about various ethnic/racial groups, or about occupations. I ask student what they know, from their own lived experiences, what is "true" about these same identities, noting in particular how our social identities influence what we have heard or experienced to be "true" about all social identities.

For example, a person who identifies as Latino, male, and straight is going to have different "truths" about what it means to occupy the position of a gay man than would a person who identifies as Latino, male, and gay. We talk about how sometimes a person's lived experience falls outside of what most folks think is "true" and how sometimes those folks get together with others to assert the alternative "truths" they have formulated from their lived experience. For example, if, like Vincente, both men in the above example grew up in a neighborhood that constructs gay men as "white, feminine, and morally dirty," the man who identifies as gay will have a lived experience as gay and Latino that falls outside this normative "truth" in the neighborhood, whereas the man who identifies as straight may not have any conscious lived experience of gay men at all and will therefore adhere to the normative "truth" he's learned in the neighborhood. The man who identifies as gay may well find others whose lived experience falls outside this normative "truth" as well, as Vincente did when he joined the Bureau, and create alternative "truths."

In the mainstream comp classes I have taught, students have identified normative "truths" about people who use marijuana, noting that DARE and other drug education organizations claim that those who use marijuana are victims bound to use "harder drugs" and are at high risk for death or brain damage. Students talk about how that has rarely been their lived experience of using marijuana or knowing others who do. We talk about how the people, like themselves, with lived experiences regarding those who use marijuana that are counter to the normative "truths" have created alternative "truths" and formed organizations like Cannabis Reform that work to decriminalize or legalize marijuana use.

"Draw Your Family" is an exercise that also assists students in sorting normative "truths" from the media about family from alternative "truths." Using crayons to draw their families, as I emphasize that there is no "wrong way" to do so, students create representations of their families (often nuclear or single-parent, sometimes extended including relatives and friends). Students share these drawings in small groups, noting the specific differences and similarities between how they represent their families and the composition of their families as well as the composition of other people's families. I ask students to then draw the family they see as most represented in the media—ads, movies, magazines, and the like. Again I ask students to share their drawings and this time come to consensus about how to describe this most-represented family. We then explore as a large group the normative "truths" about families and the specific alternative "truths" based in each person's lived experience of family.

I guide students to consider then how these normative "truths" have in some way misrepresented who they or their family or someone close to them is—in other words, I ask students to look for a lived experience from their own lives that falls outside a normative "truth." It may be a time when something they did or said fell outside a normative "truth" and they noticed it or someone else pointed it out to them. Or it may be a time where they encountered someone whose behavior fell outside a normative "truth" they had learned. At times I've used visual representations of lived experience, social identity, storying, and "truths" from normative and alternative discourses to assist students in conceptualizing the relationships between these ideas.

Following these exercises with a reading about social identity development and socialization in relation to "truths" or social norms assists students in seeing how their "truths" have been shaped by normative discourses. Bobbie Harro's ten-page essay "The Cycle of Socialization" includes diagrams that explain and show Harro's theory of socialization. She delineates a number of stages and how we learn social norms and learn to either transform or reproduce those norms:

- The beginning: naive, no knowledge of norms
- First socialization: first learning of norms from family
- Institutional and cultural socialization: second learning of norms from institutions
- Results: the realization that some of the norms we hold create inequitable conditions for some while privileging others
- Actions: reproducing the status quo or the norms we know or challenging and transforming inequitable norms that perpetuate racism, sexism, heterosexism, classism, and so on

The essay appeals to students because it explains how we learn the "truths" we live by, clearly emphasizing that no one chooses the social identities a person is born into, nor do people get to choose the norms they learn. The article ends by giving practical suggestions on how individuals can join collectively to address and transform norms that drive inequitable conditions.

Rita Hardiman and Bailey Jackson's essay on social identity development, "Conceptual Foundations for Social Justice Courses," covers similar topics, elaborating on the stages of social identity development and the differences in this development based on whether one is focused on the "agent" or "target" identities one occupies. Both articles note that most people occupy both agent and target identities simultaneously and that individuals move through stages as their identities develop, introducing students to the idea of intersectionality, that identity is fluid and multiple. Students see how their own lived experiences often fall outside those normative "truths" and how those normative "truths" can and do perpetuate misrepresentations of entire groups of people who share common social identities. Beginning here, where students can identify how their own lived experiences fall outside of normative "truths," assists students in understanding the concept of performing multiple identities and the relationship of performing identity to multiple "truths."

This series of assignments creates an experience parallel to that of students on the Bureau—an opportunity for students to examine their own social identities in relation to the "truths" normative discourse purports about these identities. As students use these exercises to story their experiences and name the "truths" that shape their experience of themselves and others, we begin to discuss explicitly how to use this information to create ethos and specific identity performances and to produce writing that is meant to do something in the world. The section that follows discusses how to guide students to explicitly name the identity-based values that guide their own performance of identity as well as their audiences' performances.

### *Identity-Based Values: Guiding Students to Address Differences*
The first step in guiding students to address the important and enduring differences between themselves and others is to have students identify their own identity-based values. For the first essay of the semester, I ask students for a story that illustrates their earliest, most difficult or most successful experience as a writer and then to

analyze and interpret that story—in essence, I ask them to occupy the
position of writer and expert on their own experience and to teach
us about themselves as writers and their relationship to writing and
by extension about their identity-based values. Students have often
noted to me that this first essay assignment helps them to claim some
authority. A number of students have said to me, "I liked this assignment because I was writing about my own experience and couldn't
be wrong." Because students are typically able to tell a good story or
see how they could easily create a more vivid story, the assignment
calls attention to their competence. Esmerelda Van Dam described
her most memorable writing experience in an essay entitled "Experiences in Print." The excerpts below include the opening story and
a bit of her closing analysis. In these excerpts, note the ease with
which Esmerelda takes up the positions of writer and expert on her
own experience and the salience of identity-based values implicit in
the excerpt.

> The writing experience that really sticks out for me is the
> time I wrote my first movie review for a local newspaper. . . .
> It was a dreadfully frosty morning in mid-February last year
> and I wasn't exactly excited about getting up extra early to
> open the office for nine o'clock. I worked for *Pride News
> Magazine,* a local Caribbean newspaper in Toronto that my
> dad owns. . . . My dad handed me a free pass to see the new
> movie *Down to Earth* starring Chris Rock. . . . I went to see
> the movie the next day and had a blast. . . . I sat wide-eyed
> at my computer for the next two days and enthusiastically
> mixed together the factual content from the movie with my
> own opinions on it. . . . This event helped me to see my
> writing abilities in a different light. Now I feel that, not only
> if I'm interested in what I'm writing, but also if I make it
> interesting by putting more of myself and more effort into
> what I do, then I can be as great a writer as I want to be.

Here Esmerelda weaves her multiple identities as writer, newspaper columnist, Canadian, and member of the Caribbean Canadian
community with the identity-based values of a person who values fun,

writing, and expressing her own opinions. Though most students do not include the kind of analysis and interpretation of their stories that meet my identity-based values as an academic reader, I can speak to this absence in terms of differences in cultural "truths" and conventions rather than as a lack of talent on the students' part (Bartholomae, Fox, and Newkirk also speak to framing what students know or don't know as cultural differences). Tom Newkirk notes the importance of clearly identifying and valuing the cultural "truths" students draw upon to formulate their ideas and compose their essays, even if those cultural "truths" result in essays that David Bartholomae and Anthony Petrosky call "lessons in life," homilies meant to educate the reader. Though the lesson in life genre is not valued in the academy, we can acknowledge the value of this genre and the identity-based values in mainstream culture and introduce students to the identity-based values and conventions that are valued in the academy. Rather than dismiss and devalue literary genres valued in mainstream culture, we can do as Tom Fox suggests and simply frame these differences as differences in culture regarding what is an acceptable or valuable genre and what is not. We can guide students into contrasting those mainstream conventions with what is valued in the academy in general and in English departments in particular.

For example, we discuss the difference between writing an essay that gives advice or a lesson (something students know how to do because it is valued in mainstream media) with an essay that complicates the issues and leaves readers with questions to consider. Just last semester, several students said to me, "Tell us again about the lesson versus the question," with an air of researchers intent on understanding this new culture and the identity-based values of an audience of college professors they found themselves writing for. I emphasize that students are already experts on mainstream culture and conventions and can build on that expertise, inviting them to become experts on academic culture and conventions.

By the end of the semester, most students look back on their first essays with an academic reader's eye and are able to articulate "truths" about "good" academic discourse. In her portfolio review essay, Esmerelda comments on "Experiences in Print":

I liked most that the piece was humble in tone and it was reasonably descriptive which helped the reader get acquainted with me. What I like least was how it sounded like a play-by-play at times in which I was telling events which can get boring. . . . When I completed "Experiences in Print" I was able to see what level I was at as a writer and what key things I needed to work on.

By the time Esmerelda wrote her reflective essay for the portfolio, she had internalized a number of key identity-based values important to academic writers and readers, weaving them with her own identity-based values, such as humility. The main thing Esmerelda did learn in the remaining essays, besides description, was the sort of analysis I wanted as an academic reader. She spoke to analysis directly when she described what she learned in writing her final essay, a research paper about the sporting industry: "Finally, 'Bouncing Lemons and Sports Fans' was a more complicated essay to write, as I had to do a lot of research including my own survey and analyzing the data to support an idea."

Building on this notion of identity-based values in academic culture, I introduce essay assignments that ask for another convention valued in the academy, close readings of published authors. Though it is not necessarily an identity-based academic value to emphasize cooperation rather than competition, I hook close reading to listening and cooperation. Doing so is an important step in creating just communities, inside and outside the classroom. Further, doing so invites students to perform another important identity, that of citizen-academic. Mary Rose O'Reilly's *The Peaceable Classroom* has been a key text for me in developing this assignment, as has Marshall Rosenberg's *Nonviolent Communication . . . A Language of Compassion*. Krista Ratcliffe's idea of rhetorical listening, "turning intent back on the listener, focusing on listening with intent, not for it" (220), has also helped in this assignment.

I teach close readings as a kind of conversation about ideas between "I and thou" (an idea used by Rosenberg and popularized by Martin Buber). Using Peter Elbow's idea of text-wrestling, I invite students to take authority *with* rather than authority *over* the published authors. This framing invites students to become fellow thinkers and academics as I teach them how to come into conversation with published authors, honoring their own piece of "truth" as well as what is "true" for the published authors.

This is perhaps the most difficult assignment. The ideas in the published essays are typically from an identity-based value system unfamiliar to students and written in an academic dialectic that is equally unfamiliar, and I call for students to sort their reactions from what the author says and not conflate the two. Students' initial reactions to the published authors are often, "This author is just wrong; he doesn't know what he's talking about!" or more specifically, "The author is biased, a racist! Why are we reading this?" I encourage students to follow these strong emotional reactions, asking them to name the feeling (are they confused or annoyed?) and what they are needing (clarity and understanding or self-expression—to voice their own view?) or what values of theirs are apparently in conflict with the authors' ideas. The next step is to guide students to look closely at what each published author is actually saying and ask, What are the "truths" in the text? What are the evaluations you as a reader bring to the text; what "truths" are you applying? I ask students to hang on to what they need as readers and note what stories from their own lives are evoked by the published authors; I tell them that these stories will be key in creating an authentic conversation between themselves and the published authors. I advise students in my classes to "try to hold in mind that you and the authors each have a piece of the truth, and none of us has the whole truth."

What I notice next as we discuss how to accurately portray the authors' "truths" in conversation with the students' "truths" is a palpable sense of relief in the students as they realize they neither have to agree and submit or disagree and rebel. Instead, they begin to take up the position of authority-with and create a dialogue with the published authors about the ideas in the text.

I invite students to represent this conversation with published authors in a number of different frames—a fictional correspondence with the authors, a fictional talk show, a personal narrative that references the authors' ideas explicitly, or an academic style paper (see appendix A, essay 2).

Jena Thomas chose to create a fictional correspondence between herself and Eli Clare, author of "The Mountain," and Thomas Frank, author of "Why Johnny Can't Dissent." The excerpts below show how Jena took up authority-with and invited the authors to speak back to her in her opening fictional letter to both of them. Note how Jena chose to use Frank's and Clare's first names and in turn had them refer to her by her first name. I see this as a way Jena created an authority-with position as she discussed with them the relevant "truths" she was exploring:

Eli and Thomas,

Both your articles forced me to think about the way society functions and acts as well as reacts towards rebellion. . . . Each of you has very individual outlooks upon the notion of rebellion. I feel that I lie somewhere in the middle between the two. While no one is truly dissenting from society, perhaps a person can pave the way for a total change in the way society thinks.

Jena went on to introduce an experience she had on a music tour and to reflect on the nature of rebellion, using both Clare's and Frank's "truths" or "outlooks" on rebellion as a lens to re-see the tour.

At the Vans Warped Tour I thought about both your papers. Eli, you discuss . . . society's labels for people. I found myself both labeling others and myself. Amongst all the labeling I realized that at this concert, the tables are turned. The "freaks" were more "normal" or rather in the majority and I, usually in the majority, dressed in shorts and a T-shirt, was in fact part of a severe minority; and I became the "freak" in the crowd. I was forced to think about how much of what these people stood for . . . anti-consumerism, etc. was paradoxical. While they hated to be part of a group or a trend, they were in fact, part of one, buying all the products to be part of that trend. I feel this is what you are trying to illustrate, Thomas, that consumerism prevents anyone from being as different from others in society as they would like to think they are.

Speaking back to herself as Eli Clare, Jena concluded her fictional correspondence with what were clearly her own new understandings about the nature of rebellion, what was now "true" about rebellion for Jena.

> Rebellion can't be about what others think; it must be about breaking a person's own rules as well as defying the standards society sets.

This sort of close reading assignment offers students the opportunity to deliberate ideas with others who hold different identity-based values in a context where no one need be "right" and where the goal is to instead understand and critically think with others. This is the first step in making allies and becoming an ally.

### Moving Audiences: Occupying the Role of Ally

There is much complex material in the field on "personal writing," such as Candace Spigelman's award-winning article in *College English,* "Argument and Evidence in the Case of the Personal." Spigelman states that we need to find ways to present personal experience as a means of argument. I propose that we work in our writing classrooms to ground the construction of ethos in personal experience. I suggest that we invite the students in our classes to begin the project of changing their audience's thinking about a specific issue by exploring the connection between their own identity-based values, their audiences' identity-based values, and the issue. Once students are connected to the issues in their own stories, we can use those stories to assist students in thinking about identity as performed for a public purpose.

Both the open letter and the research paper I assign (see appendix A, essays 3 and 4) begin with inviting students to remember events in their own lives and to connect those events to the public world. The open letter begins with experiential exercises students have done in class with others and is followed by prompts that are meant to be done at home or privately in class. At times I have asked students to use their journals to record their answers to these prompts (journals I never read, though I count the pages in front of them at the beginning of class once a week and give credit for the number of pages to encourage participation). I know from discussing private writing with the student speakers that this assignment does not eliminate imagining an audience that cannot and does not allow students to articulate experiences that fall outside of normative "truths." I also know from these same student speakers that sometimes this imagined audience invites and expects to hear about those events that fall outside the norms.

More than once I have conferenced with an anxious student who wanted to write about an issue based on a painful personal experience and was afraid of becoming too vulnerable by revealing it in the first person. In those cases, the student and I worked to develop two rhetorical identities—one a persona the student writer claimed as her own and the second a persona or a "friend" who had experienced this painful event (see Herrington and Curtis for another example of students using this strategy). In these cases, the students preserved their anonymity and were able to address their peers on an issue central to their own lives in way that satisfied them.

The goal of the prompts is for students to list as many moments from their lived experiences as they can privately, on their own. For example, I ask, "When did you first realize you were a boy or a girl or recognize your family members' gender identities?" or, "When did you first realize others assumed things about you or your family that you thought were not true?"

Once students have a list, I ask them to select two experiences and story them, describing in detail each situation. At times I have asked students to hold in mind that situation and lead the class on a guided imagery meditation. In this two-minute meditation, I ask students to put themselves back in that moment and to note as many sensory details as possible. When I stop the meditation, I have students write for ten minutes all the details they just imagined. I have seen this technique used in various writing workshops, though the first time I was introduced to it was in a workshop for hospice volunteers to help them develop the needed empathy for the people with whom they'd be working. Volunteers were asked to imagine that they too had been given a six-month terminal diagnosis. I continue to be struck by the power of such a simple guided meditation to evoke vivid details and create a strong pathetic appeal when used in an essay (see appendix B).

Helen Lao incorporated the writing she did in response to the guided imagery meditation for her open letter. This piece was to her future daughter, Vivian, a little girl she imagined would need guidance particularly about gender roles for girls. Helen told Vivian memory, a vivid lesson in the power of gender role norms:

> I remember a time when I was around seven years of age. Bored with the quietness of a small town, my buddies and I went to the train tracks to hit trains as they sped by. The sound of the sticks against metal and our shouting brought our parents to the scene. The parents of the boys were not as angered by this act, but my mom's face flamed as she yelled into my face. I remember her telling me a girl should be pretty, not dirty; quiet rather than loud and obnoxious; and obedient rather than wild. Neither your grandmother nor I realized that by punishing my wildness, we were taking away part of who I was. I guess we were too focused on me becoming a good girl that is portrayed in mainstream media.

In this passage, Helen was able to show, through her lived experience and analysis of that experience, how we enforce those norms or "truths" about what it means to be a "good" girl. Helen went on to reassure her daughter and the wider audience that she would not participate in punishing people for acting outside of their prescribed gender roles, implicitly offering her audience the role of an ally willing to support her decision:

> I want to tell you that you will never be suppressed for doing things that are too un-girlish. If it is part of who you are, there is nothing wrong with it. . . . Vivian, always remember that I love you, and I will always accept you.
>
> Your Mother,
>
> Helen

Helen's letter is an example of how I work with students to articulate their personal experiences as stories and to connect those stories to the principles of specific identity performance they have learned in experiential exercises. I ask students to identify "normative truths" and "alternative truths" in their stories and to note the relationship of those concepts to the "lived experience" they have just storied. I encourage students to examine how these "truths" position them and to pay particular attention to the differing "identities" they create on paper. As students move to revising this essay into an open letter, often students include their analysis and interpretation implicitly.

Alisa De Los Santos sent one such letter to her younger sister, Yudiana. In the excerpts below, Alisa takes on the roles of mentor and citizen, examining the impact of sexism on her life for the benefit of her sister:

> Yudiana,
>
> I would like you to know that being comfortable with who you are is a fortunate privilege for many people. . . . Our parents immigrated to the United States many years ago in search of the supposed American dream. In society race and gender affect the quality of our lives in every aspect. While attending school I remember how the boys were always picked on to answer the math problems. . . . Experiences like this have limited my ability in math. Our home environment also has interrupted my interest in math; Junior was always expected to do better in math, while I was expected to do better in verbal subjects. Growing up with an older brother exposed me to the normalizing truths society sets on women.

Using her own lived experience as well as readings on normalizing truths and socialization, Alisa took up the position of educator and mentor. She showed through her descriptions how Junior had been positioned as a math expert simply because he was male and how she had been positioned as a "better in verbal subjects" simply because she was female. Alisa used this letter to show her younger sister that there is more than just one "truth" regarding aptitude for particular subjects and biological sex and invited Yudiana to question how these "normalizing truths" were shaping her own opportunities.

Before they do their last revision on the open letter, we read James Baldwin's "Letter to My Nephew." We use the concepts above as a lens to identify where Baldwin stories his lived experience and references his and others' social identities as well as normative and alternative "truths." When I ask students what they notice, invariably they see how specifically Baldwin uses stories to articulate his and other people's identities as well as the competing "truths" black and white folks espouse.

It is at this juncture that I introduce the classical concepts of ethos, pathos, and logos, connecting each concept with a concept from specific identity performance theory students have been learning. In particular, we recall how ethos is about autonomy and agency and also about those "truths" that shape what we can and cannot imagine or do. We pay close attention to Baldwin performing his own identity through personal stories and references to these "truths." We discuss how Baldwin creates a believable ethos, an identity on paper through the use of stories that reveal differing social identities as uncle, brother, son, black man, and citizen. We look at how Baldwin uses quotes from a respected white author (Charles Dickens) and the Holy Bible, references that further situate him as an insider to both white and black culture. We also note how he positions his nephew and his audience—his nephew as an expert on the black experience of discrimination and poverty and as a compassionate person and a guide and the white audience as "lost younger brothers" ignorant of the suffering of the black community.

We identify how Baldwin uses logos, appealing to reason, to highlight the contrast between the normative white "truth" and the alternative black "truth" about race and opportunity in the United States. Students also note how Baldwin stories his lived experiences for pathos, appealing to emotion with descriptive passages.

It is with Baldwin's open letter in mind that students return to their own letters and revise, attending to the way they position themselves and the members of their audience. I ask them to strive again to develop an "I-thou" relationship with all audience members, noting their own identity-based needs and values and those of their varied audience, leaving off judgment and criticism in favor of observations and naming conflicting strategies for meeting identity-based needs and values. I coach students to articulate a request they have of their audiences, something concrete. For example, one student last semester wrote to a friend about the friend's use of the word "fag" and asked that friend to consider the consequences of using that word and to consider how he might express himself in a different way.

Drafting a letter from the essay brings the notion of audience, particularly the wider audience that may or may not hold views consonant with the student's, vividly to mind. Just as the Bureau's guidelines for considering audience provoke conversation among student speakers, we have similar discussions in my own classroom about audience awareness. Though we don't talk about ourselves as educators per se, we work at recognizing and addressing those that hold values antithetical to our own. I do guide students to ask themselves, "How am I going to get that person to hear my values, what's important to me, without alienating or jeopardizing my connection to that person?"

Having the students address the open letter to a younger person they care about can assist them in steering clear of language that blocks communication (see Rosenberg's ideas about how moralistic judgments, denying responsibility, demands, and inferring that some deserve punishment and others reward block communication). Asking them to recall editorials they have read that triggered anger, shame, or embarrassment can also help students identify language that is not likely to invite dialogue and identification. In his portfolio review, Jim Taylor noted how he struggled in the open letter to communicate to an audience whose views were antithetical to his own.

> My second essay was a letter to a person I despised for a long time. . . . My first draft of this essay was obscene. My professor put it best when she suggested to change the letter from a rant into a dialogue, something that posed questions Vicki could respond to. She encouraged me to engage in a discussion that would further both my point of view and Vicki's. . . . My final draft not only lacked strong, hateful emotions the first draft carried, but also stated how I felt and what I felt needed to be done.

We use ethos to create roles for our audiences, inviting audience members to become who we want them to be rather than castigating them for who they are or are not (similar to the work that both

Burke and Booth and many others do). We compare the sort of inflammatory editorials that most of us are familiar with to the goal I set for us: to produce writing that invites an indifferent or hostile audience into a conversation about the values important to us. Dialogue becomes central. I use exercises that assist students in taking up and trying on a variety of viewpoints in order to incorporate and speak from multiple perspectives as they write.

The most compelling reason to enter dialogue is to discuss that which is most personally important to us, and to that end, as in the Bureau training workshops, I invite students to explore the texts of their lived experiences. Esmerelda Van Dam noted in her portfolio review the value of using personal experience for a public issue in an open letter format:

> I was able to discuss a serious social issue and how it affected my life and those I care about. . . . This letter allowed me to become very personal and relate to the audience. I was able to tie in my developing skills in using descriptive language and personal experience to speak logically about an important issue. . . . I learned that I could be a very impactful and believable writer.

The open letter leads easily to a research assignment on a community issue that concerns students and one community to which they belong (see appendix A, essay 4). By framing a research paper in this way and teaching students to do their own primary research in the form of surveys or interviews, we can position students as researchers and again as citizens.

I ground my teaching of this essay assignment in Ken Macrorie's idea of "I-search" rather than "re-search." This assignment asks students to put the issues important to their communities at the center and to narrate the process of their search for strategies that might address these issues. I invite students to create a dialogue, to locate differing viewpoints on their issue, and to name constituents that embody those viewpoints with the goal of selecting two of those viewpoints and then describing each one, including the students' own.

In the process of writing this essay, students identify how these constituents position themselves and critically analyze those people's identity-based needs and values, identifying what strategies these constituents use to address the issue. Students do the same for themselves, clearly naming the strategies they prefer and noting how these strategies reflect the way they are positioned, their own identity-based needs and values.

Kevin Murray, a student who had struggled to articulate his concerns in my writing class, took the opportunity offered in this assignment to investigate an issue personally important to him: people's attitudes toward IV drug users and needle exchange. As Kevin surveyed his peers about the issue, he noticed that people asked him again and again, "How would this reduce the problem of drug addiction in America?" In his essay, Kevin explained that needle exchange has nothing to do with reducing the drug problem in America; instead, he writes, "The intention of the needle exchange . . . is to provide addicts with a safe and cheap way to shoot up, free of disease."

Kevin went on to describe the life of his cousin, a twenty-three-year-old heroin addict, and what Kevin hoped needle exchange would do for his cousin:

> His life is horrible and hard to deal with as it is. But, of course, things could be worse. I'm convinced the only way life could be worse for him is if he contracted . . . HIV. . . . So, what's the practice of needle exchanging going to do for my cousin, and other addicts across America? Hopefully give him a safe way to shoot up while he tries to get help and get clean; give him some leeway time.

As Kevin related what politicians have said about the issue, he noted that opponents of needle exchange see it as a moral issue and seem to not see addicts as human beings who need help. In his conclusion, Kevin took up the identity of a concerned citizen:

> The people of this country need to start being more concerned about these problems and begin to see the whole

> picture. In actuality people are dying: adults, kids, brothers, sisters, mothers, and friends. All of them are dying and it has nothing to do with how bad or how good that person ever was in life. . . . The bottom line is that people need help. . . . The point of needle exchange . . . is to give addicts time to come to terms with themselves. I wish people could see through all that and make it okay.

Here we see Kevin getting specific, complicating what it means to be an addict, as he positions addicts as "adults, kids, brothers, sisters, mothers, and friends," an alternative "truth."

Kevin asserted that addicts are human beings and used his lived experience as a family member of an addict to position himself as an informed and concerned citizen. In doing so, Kevin offered ally positions for his audience to occupy. He offered needle exchange as a strategy that would meet the needs of those addicted to IV drugs and those who care about them, inviting his audience to become some of the people who are interested in seeing addicts have a chance to "come to terms with themselves."

I coach students, in ways similar to those Krista Ratcliffe explains in her article "Rhetorical Listening: A Trope for Interpretive Invention and a 'Code of Cross-Cultural Conduct,'" asking them to simply lay out the differing viewpoints around the issue and "listen with intent, not for it" (220) before they attempt to advocate for a particular strategy. Luisa Santiago, a student who had struggled with narrative as well as analysis in college writing, chose drug dealing in her home community as the issue she wanted to address in her I-search paper. She began by clearly identifying the problem and those whose lives were touched by this issue.

> The issue of drug dealing in downtown Holyoke, MA is a very important issue to me and to the people of my community. This problem effects numerous people, including myself, and even little children, many of whom are getting hurt because of it. Some may get shot because of a deal with a bad customer; others may get dealt drugs that will kill them once taken. It is important to me because I know people and have

friends that deal drugs and I want to see it stopped before they get hurt, even if [it] means they must be punished.

Luisa paid particular attention to those who deal drugs and their neighbors, noting, "Drug dealing for some people is a way of meeting their everyday needs. It causes a lot of problems for the community and now they [the neighbors] have an unmet need for safety." Quoting her transcript of her interview with a local drug dealer, Luisa detailed the everyday needs people meet by dealing drugs. When Luisa asked the young man who deals drugs why he thought people start dealing, he answered:

> Respect mostly, and to fit into the neighborhood. If you deal drugs where I live, you're looked up to and treated with respect. Also it is a good way to stay safe; your people will protect you once you get on their side. And what I said before, money. You get a lot of it. . . . That's the main reason I do it. . . . As for my family, they don't really like it. . . . If you're asking if they like disown me or something the answer is no. I do have some friends where their families have thrown them out, but that's not me. I haven't really gotten into any really serious trouble, I'm good like that.

Using this excerpt assisted Luisa in humanizing the position of drug dealer, an alternative "truth." She followed this interview excerpt with her own story, how she witnessed a stabbing that was a direct result of a drug deal gone bad:

> It was an obvious conversation about drugs and this really terrified me. The man got really harsh and started threatening my friend's brother and all of a sudden the man took out a knife and stabbed him and ran off. . . . The stab wasn't bad luckily and he survived.

Again, Luisa was able to humanize those who are dealing drugs and those like herself who are traumatized by the violence that often accompanies dealing. Luisa connected her own primary research and experience with what she was able to learn about agencies that address drug abuse with the published story of a young man who, with a counselor's help, was able to drop drug dealing as a way of life. In the end, Luisa called for home education about drug use and community meetings as a way to address drug dealing. Luisa offered her audience roles to play as active community members willing and able to address the drug dealing issue and ended her essay by reminding us, "People's lives are at stake and no one wants to lose the people they love and care about most."

Using identity-based or personal writing in the classroom need not become an exercise in solipsistic confession. Students in the first-year required classes I taught were able to use their lived experiences to think critically about social justice and to participate in social action. These first-year students did so in assignments that asked them to

- name the positions they took up or were assigned or assigned to others,
- identify the differing and contingent "truths" that guide them and others,
- negotiate their own and others' multiple identities and concomitant identity-based values,
- and create invitations, roles for their audiences to take up as allies willing to work with them to address issues in their communities.

Reflecting on specific identity performance in relation to communities and social justice problematizes students' reliance on stereotypes and helps them see themselves as allies to more causes than those with which they primarily identify, as I show in earlier chapters. In the final chapter, I trace my own trajectory, how writing this book and reflecting on specific identity performance has helped me to frame a number of classroom initiatives that further address the issues of becoming an ally and making allies in the service of rhetorical development and social justice. In the process, I'll invite us to consider the roles of writing teachers as citizens and as those who mentor citizens.

# 5 / Making Allies in the Community

**As** I began this final chapter, my government chose to use war as a strategy to get its needs met for what I imagine to be safety, respect, and justice. While I share these needs, staging war in Iraq does not meet my needs for safety, respect, and justice for all, nor does the strategy of war resonate with my valuing of nonviolence. Writing this manuscript is a strategy, a call to action that works for me. As I edited this book, I re-read Mary Rose O'Reilly's *The Peaceable Classroom*, written in 1993, and I was struck with her references to the aftermath of the Gulf War (another war, another George Bush) and her repetition of her mentor Ihab Hassan's question: Can we teach English so that people stop killing each other? My own question is, Can we teach writing so that people use language for social justice, including safety and justice for all world citizens?

The problems we have been contemplating are how to encourage rhetorical growth using a pedagogy based on specific identity performance and, further, how to teach writing for social justice. How do we as writing teachers teach social justice in a way that invites students to become participating citizens in the communities to which they belong? In other words, how do we as rhetoricians help students locate their multiple identities in context, identify "truths" from a variety of ideologies, value ally-building, and begin the work of addressing problematic community issues? I suggest that we as teachers of writing become willing to model this work for the students in our classrooms, just as the student speakers on the Speaker's Bureau model ally-building and invite their audiences to become allies with them to address the pervasive homophobia and heterosexism on campus. And as student speakers do, it is important that we as teachers

locate, carefully select, and share some of our own multiple identities and the identity-based "truths" we hold (those values that we
have come to believe in relation to our social identities through our
primary and secondary socializations and our cultural, family, and
personal histories and experiences). We can choose to perform both
insider and outsider identities and, like the student speakers, to occupy the role of ally with students and create roles for students to take
as allies with us. In this way we can model ally-building, an ability
to dialogue across disparate values in search of common ground.

We can begin to model the work of addressing community issues
through deliberation as student speakers do in their panel presentations: connect with students by striving to understand their points
of view and actively respond to them as well as introduce new knowledge, new discourses, and "truths" in order to build knowledge with
students. The trajectory of my work with specific identity performance
(grounded in what I have learned from my study of speakers on the
Bureau), deliberative community dialogues, and the principles of nonviolent communication[6] have led me to develop an ethic for those of
us interested in teaching social justice, modeling ally-building, and
community problem solving in the writing classroom. The four principles of this ethic are:

- Self-reflection: reflecting on, identifying, and discussing
  with students our own identity-based values and taking
  responsibility for our own context-bound, identity-based
  values without resorting to a transcendental "truth" or notions of right and wrong
- Separation of judgments from observations: separating the
  identity-based "truths" that we and others live by from what
  we are actually hearing or seeing and, further, identifying
  the values and needs underlying our judgments and the
  judgments of others
- Use of dialogue: attempting to confirm through dialogue
  the identity-based values and needs of others (students,
  speakers, published authors, etc.), particularly those who
  hold differing positions and opinions
- A focus on making allies and common ground: focusing
  on our common values and needs by separating our own

and others' identity-based values from the many possible
strategies or approaches to an issue that might satisfy us
as well as those we wish to work with

I am suggesting that we as teachers of writing need to walk
these ethics—performing our identities as in-flux and multiple; modeling ally behavior and ally-making; and reminding ourselves and
students that though we all have an important piece of the context-
bound "truth" about a community issue, none of us alone can divine
the whole picture.

It is not easy to practice these ethics; I have often found it nearly
impossible to consistently use them as a teaching practice. Nevertheless, when I have been able to remember that my own needs cannot
be met at the expense of the needs of others—to practice self-reflection, separation of observations from judgments, deep listening, and
a focus on common ground, employing humility and compassion—
I see the learning that happens for both myself and the students.

So, what does it look like to practice these ethics and model ally-
building and community problem solving in the classroom? I am thinking of one particular day last fall, the first day of class: as I handed
out the first assignment, a student said loudly enough for all of us
to hear, "This is bullshit," as he glared down at the paper in his hand.
In the silence that followed, students looked from me to the student
who had spoken.

My first thought was, "These students have no sense of audience!"
matching the student's judgment with my own, shifting the blame
from myself back to him. I slowed down and realized that what I was
wanting was some respect; I wondered what he was wanting. I asked
him if he felt overwhelmed and was wanting some clarity on what I
was expecting, and he said yes. I told him we were going to go over
the assignment slowly. He seemed satisfied.

I didn't leave it there, though; I decided to teach him a lesson
and said, "See how much easier it would've been if you had said you
were overwhelmed and needed help understanding the assignment?"

Next class he came in swearing. Again I guessed at his feelings
and needs; I learned he was exhausted and overwhelmed with the
first few days of school, missing home and home-cooked food. This
time I refrained from teaching him a lesson, and class went on. Af-

ter class I asked him to stay. And he guessed what I was wanting: respect. I told him I wanted both of us to have respect, and I want folks to feel safe in our classroom. He promised not to swear anymore, and as he left he smiled and asked, "Can I tell the other kids I told you to fuck off?"

I snorted aloud, amused and delighted we could joke about what could have been the beginning of a very unpleasant semester for both of us, and said, "Whatever you need to do." By mid-semester he wrote me a letter about how important it had been for him to know me and work with me, and I wrote him back, telling him how much I had learned from him about teaching.

As Robert Brooke notes in his essay "Underlife and Writing Instruction," these sorts of responses, both mine and the student's, are part of the underlife of any classroom. The student and I were challenging, at first in a contained way, the institutionally assigned roles for "student" and "teacher" and creating what Brooke calls "individual stances towards the classroom experience" (144). My response, what Brooke would call a disruptive form of underlife, was to invite a dialogue about what both the student and I were wanting from our shared writing workshop. According to Brooke, "Writing instruction seeks to help the learner see herself as an original thinker, instead of a 'student' whose purpose is to please teachers by absorbing and repeating information" (152). In other words, teaching writing is about inviting students to examine and explore the roles or identities they are performing and the ideologies they are creating, reproducing, or resisting in relation to those identities. Like Brooke's theory of underlife, my own theory of specific identity performance suggests that "we think carefully about the identities we have, the identities we model, and the identities we ask students to take on, for the process of building identity is the business we are in" (152).

Ethos, the performance of specific and multiple identities in order to make allies around issues and effect change, is at the center of my ethics for teaching social justice. Ethos-building depends on what I say and do, how I create roles to take as an ally to the students, and how I offer students roles to take as my allies. Like the student speakers, I come into the classroom with the social identities of expert and educator, identities conferred on me and valued by the institution. On the other hand, the way I dress signals the social identity of an outsider, a nonconformist, someone who chooses to ignore the usual dress codes for "professors" and "women." I choose to dress casually, often in jeans and boots; my face is free of makeup; I wear my thick salt-and-pepper hair cropped short, revealing my light olive complexion; and the tattoo on my right forearm is often visible when I teach. I am as conscious of my manner and dress as any of the student speakers on the Bureau; however, unlike Vincente and Viany, who carefully dressed to conform to culturally appropriate gender roles and to create identification between themselves and their peers, I use the way I dress to assert a new ideology about difference—and not just sexual difference, all differences.

It is the tattoo that most intrigues the present generation of students. When they ask what it says, I tell them, "It's Sanskrit for 'awakened heart' to remind me to be compassionate so that when I start pointing and giving orders, I remember to open my hand, be kind, and invite cooperation instead."

My nonconformist performance seems both to appeal to and repel students—most identify with this outsider identity because the outspoken, rugged individualist is a valued archetype in U.S. culture. The students' reactions are similar regarding my status as a professor, a valued insider—it also seems to attract and repel them. I use my insider/outsider positioning just as student speakers do, to connect with students and introduce new ideas. I build a complicated ethos that extends beyond my official roles and the way I physically represent myself. The way I conduct class introduces students to my ethics.

I respond to students, positioning myself as an attentive listener and an interested guesser, and I revisit situations that I botch. As I noted in the last chapter, from the first day of class I invite students to address me by my first name and write me "Dear Zan" letters about their experience in the class. Like student speakers, I speak for myself—claiming my observations, analyses, and interpretations from my own particular identities—in particular from the point of view of an "academic reader, a writer, and a person." In short, I complicate my ethos; I perform multiple, in-flux, often apparently conflicting, and specific identities.

I focus on common ground. In the example above, both the student and I were able to identify our common need for respect. We were able to separate our conflicting judgments about what was "true" about the assignment I handed out (was it "useful" or "bullshit"?) and drop instead into considering what we were both needing, respect. The common ground confirmed, the student and I agreed implicitly that I would not "educate" him and agreed explicitly that he would not swear in the classroom.

This experience illustrated foundational principles for me: the necessity to meet people where they are; to restrain myself from judging, comparing, or demanding; and to admit that though I may have a teaching plan I really like, I am powerless regarding how it will go over and what students are struggling with in any given day. Compassion and humility are the values I draw upon to practice teaching in this way.

For me, the process begins well before the first day of class: I make a decision to practice foregrounding connection above carrots and sticks in the belief that connection fosters learning for students as well as for teachers. I vow to practice self-reflection, striving to identify the judgments I am making about students and myself and translating those judgments into what I am observing and into values of mine that are met or unmet, such as respect, understanding, community, peace, or cooperation. I prepare myself to practice damage control by reminding myself that I can guess what students are observing and what values of theirs lurk behind the judgments they are making.

Informing my teaching practice are these principles. Before the end of the first day of class, I ask students two questions in their "Dear Zan" letter:

- What kind of a class do you want?
- What can all of us do to help you feel comfortable participating in our class?

Student answers are quite similar. Last semester in all four classes I taught, "fun" topped the list, followed closely by "respect" and "openness." Favorite strategies to meet fun, respect, and openness included small group work and discussion. The second day of class, after students answer these questions individually, I ask students to get into groups and share their responses. I give each group a list of scenarios—conflicts that have emerged in classes I have taught. These include:

- The teacher gives instructions nobody understands.
- A student falls asleep.
- Students complain there's not enough time to finish the assignment by the due date.
- A student responds to an assignment by announcing, "This is bullshit."
- A group member doesn't prepare work the group needs to do the assignment.

Students then create two role plays: a worst-case scenario, one that doesn't match what they want in their class, and a best-case scenario, one that does match the values they've articulated.

The worst-case scenario is meant for entertainment. Together we enjoy strategies we have all used to get our needs met, strategies that don't contribute to everyone's well-being. I'm recalling here a role play where a student named Jerry Smoyer became Dr. Smoyer. He addressed his "class" with a long series of convoluted instructions. When he was done, a "student" announced, "This is bullshit!" And Dr. Smoyer threw a piece of chalk at his head!

Like the lead speaker at a Speaker's Bureau panel presentation, I open a space for students to create ground rules with me. We consider together the best-case scenarios, questioning how realistic the role plays are, and discuss strategies that might work and class values, adding any values and strategies we agree upon.

I value the practice of co-writing or collaborative writing projects as a way to learn how to negotiate values within the student groups as well as between audience members and writers. I design assignments that invite students to identify their own judgments and translate those judgments into what they are observing and into what values of theirs are met or unmet. I emphasize the importance of listening deeply to one another, and without judgment, particularly to other group members whose opinions and values differ from our own. I start small, inviting students in class to draft together an opening paragraph and a title based on reading and writing they have done individually.

I ask for reflection about the process of composing together. Kathleen spoke to her new understanding of working with differences in her group in this reflection:

> At first I thought that I would need a group that had the same views and ideas on [a] particular subject to work with, but I've now learned that it's better to have a group that has many different views on ideas so the group can get a broad perspective on the issues. Everyone in the group must respect the other views and ideas that different people bring to the group. The ideas must be taken seriously and worked into the piece the group is writing so everyone in the group has a part in the writing.

After groups compose their paragraphs, they read the paragraphs aloud to the class. As the others listen, I ask students to list separately their observations—what they actually heard—and their evaluations of one another's titles and paragraphs. I list these on the board, assisting students in separating their observations from their evaluations.

Together we work to fill in what students are actually observing that leads them to a particular evaluation. For example, students evaluate a paragraph as "good" and support this evaluation with the observation that the paragraph included references to the reading and met the parameters of the assignment. Likewise, students evaluate a title as "good" and support this evaluation with the observation that the title used words that have an emotional charge and build suspense because it is not immediately obvious why the author used this title.

When I ask how this practice might be useful to them, students make the connection to peer review, noting how much more information they get when the evaluation is linked to specific observations. They also quickly realize how much easier it is to hear what their peer reviewer is wanting when that reviewer takes responsibility for his or her observations and evaluations by using "I" instead of "you should," saying, "You can see what the peer reviewer wants and

you don't feel defensive. You can think about it." This exercise enables us to see that observations are what underlie evaluations and
to experience how specific context-bound observations help writers
revise. I invite students to further think about how the audiences for
their own writing might respond when they mix their observations
about an issue with their evaluations, how the audience, like the
writers in peer review groups, might hear criticism and shut down,
becoming defensive.

Of all the collaborative assignments that have evolved from my
teaching ethics, the deliberative dialogue pamphlet has been one of
the most generative in terms of teaching students to make allies by
inviting a dialogue about a controversial issue in a way that gives student writers and their audiences opportunities to listen deeply to multiple points of view about an issue. My original impetus for this assignment was the necessity to teach a kind of perspectives essay—an
essay meant to give students the experience of writing about an issue from at least two perspectives. As I worked to form this assignment, I drew on what I had learned from the Speaker's Bureau, asking students to do the same type of rhetorical work that student
speakers do: invite dialogue about a controversial issue without resorting to transcendental "truths" or reducing issues to black and
white debates where there are winners and losers. I also used the deliberative dialogue forums and the pamphlets that go with these forums. I was first introduced to deliberative dialogue when I joined
the faculty of FPC in the fall of 2003. The New England Center for
Civic Life and its Diversity Project at FPC hold three to five deliberative dialogue forums a semester on a variety of topics. All of these
forums are open to the entire college community, first-year students
to full professors.

The ideas for forum topics emerge from problematic community
issues, sometimes called "wicked problems" because of their complex, multifaceted nature. Focus groups discuss the issue in a series
of issue-framing forums comprised of participants who have a stake
in the issue. These focus groups are guided to discuss each issue and
the tensions surrounding those issues. As members of the group
gather concerns from as many different constituents as they can,
multiple approaches emerge. Once the focus group identifies more

than two approaches, a portion of the focus group creates a pamphlet that introduces the issue and the tensions in that issue as well as three distinct approaches to that issue. For example, the Diversity Project developed the pamphlet "Sex: Public Policy for Private Passions," which introduced the tensions surrounding sexual orientation, giving some history of the gay civil rights movement and the struggle surrounding it.

- Approach 1 called for laws to protect the rights of persons of various orientations.
- Approach 2 called for a reassertion of heterosexuality as the norm.
- Approach 3 advocated for a culture that values all sexual orientations.

Each approach detailed what "Supporters Believe," "What Can Be Done," what "Critics Say," and "Trade-Offs" inherent in accepting each approach.

The deliberative dialogue forums themselves are facilitated by both student civic scholars and faculty trained to moderate deliberative dialogues. The goal of the forum is to respectfully hear many differing viewpoints, to identify any common ground, and to determine how the participants' thinking may have changed or deepened about the issue and about the approaches to that issue. Participants leave with ideas of how they individually and collectively might approach and address the issue in question. For example, in the forum I attended on "Sex," we agreed that we all wanted all people to have safety and respect. Toward that end, many of us began to think about how we or the groups we belonged to might connect with the Gay/Straight Alliance on campus.

These forums are not so different from Speaker's Bureau panel presentations: personal or lived experience is valued, participants are encouraged to speak for themselves, and the topic is a problematic community issue. Neutral moderators introduce ground rules meant to facilitate a respectful and safe forum. They begin by guiding students and other forum participants to share their personal stake in the issue at hand, speaking just for themselves. Participants are encouraged to keep in mind the diverse experiences they have just heard from one another as they consider the approaches to the issue at hand. As the moderators introduce each approach from the forum pamphlet, they encourage forum participants to listen without judgment to the particular "truths" each approach articulates, "truths" of a real segment of their own communities. The ideologies are often new to the forum participants, challenging their own deeply held beliefs. The focus of the forum is to listen deeply to one another and respond to one another regarding each approach and any new approaches that emerge in the forum. The forum closes with the moderators inviting participants to identify ways in which their own thinking has changed or deepened about the issue and approaches and from this reflective place to identify any shared common ground as well as areas of disagreement that call for more deliberation. The emphasis is on building relationship and new knowledge, new approaches that might address a community problem in a way that satisfies all participants, a task that is not likely to be accomplished in one forum.

Using the forums and the deliberative dialogue pamphlets as an inspiration, I asked groups of students in my first-year writing classes to settle on a controversial issue they wanted to address with their peers. Again, there is a parallel here with the Speaker's Bureau training workshops and with many assignments I have explained in this book: an invitation to name what it is that is personally important. Three out of the thirteen groups from four classes decided to address the drinking age, a popular subject among first-year students. The groups collaboratively produced the first draft from their own experience and knowledge. Here are excerpts from the in-class draft Amanda, Mia, Julie, Owen, and Kathleen produced.

> The drinking age in America has always been a controversial topic. There have been many different ways in the U.S. and other countries to try and find a perfect age limit for drinking. Even though there have been other ways different countries have tried that work, the U.S. still keeps the limit at 21.
>
> People that are under 21 don't feel as if this limit is fair. At age 18 a person can vote to make a difference, or buy ciga-

rettes. It makes people under the age of 21 feel inferior to people that are 21 because they basically have the same rules against them except for the drinking limit.

There are a lot of opinions on this issue so it would take a lot of time and effort to change the law.

From this in-class draft, students created guiding research questions. As they researched their topics, gathering concerns from as many different constituents as possible, I asked them to separate carefully their observations about the information they were finding from how they felt or evaluated these sources (including noting who funded research or had a Web site—we discovered a Web site created by the major liquor companies as well as a Web site that only referenced itself and was not linked into by other credible sources). After much research, drafting, and group conferencing with and without me, these students produced a deliberative dialogue pamphlet entitled "College Drinking: A Dangerous Behavior?" These are excerpts from their opening:

> There is no doubt that underage drinking is a major public health problem in the United States. In 1998 about 10.4 million drinkers were between the ages of 12 and 20. . . . The amount of students who binge drink is 44%. . . . Not only is drinking before 21 dangerous for one's health, but it is also dangerous for the people around them and the person can get him or herself into trouble in more ways than one. 8% of people admitted to having unprotected sex when drinking, while 2% said they had sex when they were too drunk to give consent. . . . 13% of college students said they were assaulted by classmates who drank too much which translates into 600,000 people which equals the entire city of Boston.
>
> Would you feel in danger if you were to be a number in one of these statistics? Would it give college students more safety to have better transportation on campuses? Have you ever wished there was a better way to drink?

The pamphlet included three approaches:

- Approach 1: Don't Change the Law, It Wouldn't Help
- Approach 2: Improve Safety on Campuses
- Approach 3: Create More Security on College Campuses

In the end, approaches 2 and 3 blended together. Nevertheless, this group's ability to name the issue and create questions and approaches that spoke to some of the tensions from the single-perspective first draft illustrates how the students in the group learned to listen to other perspectives and invite the same listening from the audience of their pamphlet.

Not all groups were as able—most students spoke to the difficulty of working in a group, identifying values they had that were unmet, focusing on the gap between what we as a class said we valued in small groups and what actually happened. Nor was it easy for students to frame their issue in a way that assisted them in developing distinct approaches, as we can see in the example above. In response, I have revised my process of teaching issue-framing—allowing more time for students to gather and identify concerns and group these concerns in a way that facilitates the emergence of more distinct approaches. The first time I taught the forum pamphlet, one group of students was unable to complete the assignment by the first deadline I set; their pamphlet was four weeks late. I am still revising this assignment and am running it again, certain I will learn much more each time I do so. Again, this is not an easy practice, nor are these easy assignments, though I know from experience that creating and completing them is no more difficult than the work student speakers do when they enter classrooms of their peers and invite a conversation about sexual identity and civil rights to humanize the issue of homophobia and heterosexism. These practices and assignments call for patience, compassion, and often humor.

Here are the steps I took to practice and teach these ethics and the assignments guided by these ethics in my writing classroom. I offer them as suggestions for your consideration.

1. Made a decision to foreground connection above carrots and sticks in the belief that connection fosters learning for students as well as for teachers.

2. Admitted that though I could have a teaching plan I really liked, I was powerless regarding how it would go over and what students were struggling with in any given day.

3. Vowed seriously to attempt to meet students wherever they happened to be before I introduced new ideologies.

4. Continued to practice self-reflection, striving to identify the judgments I was making about students and myself and translating those judgments into what I was observing and into values of mine that were met or going unmet, such as respect, understanding, community, peace, and cooperation.

5. Practiced damage control by using self-reflection to understand my own judgments and by guessing with students what they were observing and what values of theirs lurked behind the judgments they were making.

6. Determined to revisit situations with students where self-reflection had eluded me.

7. Responded to student writing using the same principles, foregrounding connection and speaking to what I was observing in their writing that either met my values for academic writing or didn't.

8. Designed assignments that invited students to identify their own judgments and translate those judgments into what they were observing and into what identity-based values of theirs were met or unmet.

9. Encouraged students to develop more than two approaches to an issue and to practice a kind of deliberative dialogue in their group work with one another and in writing for audiences.

10. Guided students to foreground deep/rhetorical listening and the idea of making allies rather than finding allies.

11. Asked students to sort their own and their audience's identity-based values from the preferred strategies.

12. Assisted students in considering many approaches or strategies to issues that might satisfy them and their intended audiences.

I suppose you're thinking, "What an order, I can't go through with it!" These principles are meant to be suggestions only—I cannot myself claim perfection, merely progress. It is difficult to create coalitions across identity differences, to make allies in communities in order to address community issues. Yet doing so is the backbone of participatory democracy. The teaching ethic I have described and the examples of how that ethic works in practice as well as the models we have in the stories of student speakers from the Speaker's Bureau offer us as teachers of writing a way to invite the students in our classrooms to become citizens. Paradoxically, beginning with what is important personally to the students and employing assignments that make use of specific identity performance, community deliberation, and nonviolence does *not* lead to confessional, self-absorbed writing nor to the "whatever" attitude of so many disaffected youth. Instead, I have seen evidence in my classrooms that this teaching ethic encourages student engagement, curiosity, responsibility, and the growing realization in students—and in myself as a teacher—that we are each connected to one another. This is the quality I saw again and again as I observed student speakers in Bureau panel presentations—the ability to acknowledge and honor similarities and differences between themselves and their peers and to invite their peers to do the same. Clearly employing the concept of specific identity performance and the ethic for teaching that I describe as its corollary are viable ways to encourage rhetorical growth and to teach social justice in the writing classroom. Using these theories and methods as a starting point, it is my hope that we can together deliberate and create new and multiple approaches to answer Mary Rose O'Reilly's question, Can we teach English so that people stop killing each other?, and my own parallel question, Can we teach writing so that people use language for social justice for all world citizens?

Appendixes

Notes

Works Cited

Index

# Appendix A
Major Assignments

## *Essay 1: Representing Yourself as a Writer*

In this first essay, I invite you to introduce yourselves as writers. How will you represent yourself as a writer? How have the perceptions of others influenced or shaped how you feel about and what you think about yourself as a writer? Through the drafting process, you will select one story that involves writing. Tell the story and then explain what it reveals about you as a writer and explain what writing means to you. In short, you will be analyzing and interpreting that story. The point you make about writing will be unique; it will be an interpretation taken from your unique story. So, represent yourself; shape how you want us to see you as a writer. Your essays will be published in several small in-class magazines, so the audience of your essay will be our writer's workshop.

### *Exploratory Draft Begun in Class*
- Draw a picture that symbolizes how you feel about writing and then write three words that describe you as a writer.
- Make a list of what other people have told you about your writing.
- Finish the sentence "I am the kind of writer who . . ." at least ten times.
- On separate cards, list three events in which writing or reading or both were central: the first time you remember writing or reading, the most successful or easiest time you ever had reading or writing, and the most difficult or least successful time you ever had reading and writing. Then write as many details as you can remember about each event.

- Select one event and reconstruct that event in your mind and again write as many details as you can about what you remember.

### Mid-process Draft

Write an essay that includes one story, taken from your exploratory draft, as well as your interpretation of that story. Translate your experience into a story, into words—words that help your readers hear, smell, see, and feel what that event was like for you. Once you've written the story, think hard about its meaning: What did the experience mean to you at first, what does it mean to you now, and what might it mean to others, including its participants and your readers? Please don't worry about grammar and punctuation yet, and expect to find ways to revise or re-see this draft in order to write the next draft. I encourage and reward risk-taking—that means making major changes between the exploratory and mid-process drafts and between the mid-process and concluding revision drafts.

### Concluding Revision Draft

Using what you've learned from feedback/review and the exercises in revision we have done in class, revise your mid-process draft to create this draft. We will be proofreading this draft in class together. Also due: Groups will bring ideas for cover and publication art as well as drafts of tables of contents and introductions and TWO copies of the publication draft typed SINGLE-SPACED at beginning of class.

Use the proofreading help you received in class to create an error-free draft for publication. Please give your essay a title and a byline only (no need to call this "Essay 1" or write my name or the date or the class on it), and *please, please, single-space—for the sake of trees.* Paper-clip pages together, if you have more than one. Also due: Groups will bring the finished covers, table of contents, and introductions and compile copy-ready manuscripts for our first magazines.

### Portfolio

Hand in the following: one copy of the publication draft (the other is in your group's manuscript), the concluding revision draft, peer responses, the mid-process draft, the exploratory draft, and any additional notes or responses having to do with the essay. Please carefully label all but the publication drafts—these will have titles and a byline. Use the order above, publication drafts on top. When I hand these back, put all papers in your three-ring binder and return the folder to me.

*Criteria*
- Descriptive language that evokes vivid images and tells as well as shows your story
- Transitions between paragraphs and between narrating, explaining, and interpreting
- Interpretations of your story that make meaning of your story
- Tone and style that invites the audience to understand you as a writer
- A closing that leaves us with an image that helps us remember what you said about writing
- Process of revising—distinct changes between drafts
- Proofreading

### Essay 2: Representing a Conversation Between Yourself and Published Authors

In the first essay, I invited you to introduce yourselves as writers. In this second essay, I ask you to use writing to represent a conversation between yourself and the published authors we are reading in the *Original Text-Wrestling Book*. How will you represent this conversation? How will you *accurately* represent your own thoughts, ideas, feelings, and questions—your own responses to what you've read as well as to what the authors have said in their texts?

Through the drafting process, you will select a strategy to represent this conversation. You may decide to create a fictional correspondence between yourself and the author, or you may choose a story from your own life and analyze, interpret, and explain that story in light of the two readings. We will look together at the sample student essays in the book to generate more models of how to represent this conversation. Whatever way you choose to represent this conversation, I urge you to think of it as a dialogue with a friend, paying close attention to how you invite us and the published authors to seriously think about the ideas in the published essays; work at separating your observations of what the authors are saying from your evaluations and interpretations. Imagine you are able and willing to not only stand your own ground but also support the authors to stand their ground too. Work at learning *with* the authors rather than attempt to dominate them or imagine they are dominating you. Try to hold in mind that you and the authors each has a piece of the truth and none of us has the whole truth. Cultivate curiosity!

*Exploratory Draft: "The Mountain"*
For the exploratory draft, use the following questions for every two or three paragraphs of the essay:

- What do you think this piece is about?
- Where do you see this text going?
- What thoughts, associations, and/or memories are popping to mind?
- What are you feeling at this point?
- What questions do you have?

Extending the exploratory draft, consider what the author is saying:

- What are the important ideas in the text?
- How are ideas related to each other?
- What points does the author make?

*Group Response to "The Mountain" in Class*
Together your group will compose a one- to two-page response that represents the group members' differing responses to the essay as well as a clear representation of what the author is saying and will present this in class.

*Mid-process Draft: "The Mountain"*
Draw on your exploratory draft to create a fictional correspondence with the author, a series of at least three letters (three from you and three "from" the author). Be sure to include accurate representations of your own "ground" as well as the author's (700–800

words, typed). Please don't worry about grammar and punctuation yet, and expect to find ways to revise or re-see this draft in order to write the next draft. I encourage and reward risk-taking—that means making major changes between the exploratory and mid-process drafts and between the mid-process and concluding revision drafts.

*Exploratory Draft: "Why Johnny Can't Dissent"*
For the exploratory draft, use the following questions to guide your reading of the essay:

- What's this article about?
- What words and phrases catch your attention? If there are recurring images or words, what are they?
- What techniques and genres does the author use?
- How does the author present himself? What do you know about the author and his attitudes? Why is he believable or not?
- What tone do the words, techniques, and genres create?
- Who is the audience for this essay? How do you know?
- What is the purpose of this essay?

Extending the exploratory draft by adding how you feel.

- Select ten quotes that you react strongly to—either with joy, anger, confusion, etc.—and write about where those feelings take you. What other time in your own life have you felt this way?
- What stories or events in your own life come to mind as you read?
- What assumptions might you be making?
- What are you hoping for or needing as you read this essay or in relation to the topic of the essay?

*Group Response to "Why Johnny Can't Dissent" in Class*
Together your group will compose a one- to two-page response that represents the group members' differing responses to the essay as well as a clear representation of what the author is saying and will present this to the class.

*Mid-process Draft: "Why Johnny Can't Dissent"*

Draw on your exploratory draft to create an essay that tells a story from your own life and uses "Why Johnny Can't Dissent" to explain, interpret, explore, and analyze that story. Be sure to include accurate representations of your own "ground" as well as the author's (700–800 words, typed).

CONFERENCES—Classes canceled this week.

Bring BOTH mid-process drafts to the conference. We will discuss strategies for combining both into the concluding revision draft. You will receive the magazine of responses at the conference.

*Concluding Planning Note*

Sit back again, re-read everything you have written, and read the sample student essays as well as the criteria for this essay. Now, write yourself a note that explains how you will create your concluding revision draft.

*Concluding Revision Draft*

Using what you've learned from feedback/review and the exercises in revision we have done in class, revise your mid-process drafts to create this draft. Choose a strategy to represent the conversation between you and one or two of the published authors. We will be proofreading this draft in class together.

*Final Draft*

Use the proofreading help you received in class to create an error-free draft for publication. Please give your essay a title and a byline only (no need to call this "Essay 2" or write my name, date, or the class on it), and *please, please, single-space—for the sake of trees—and no cover pages.* Paper-clip pages together, if you have more than one.

*Process Note*

Use the criteria below to explain how well you met each of the criteria, noting what you are most pleased with and what you would change if you had more time. What changed between drafts? What kind of coaching do you need from me? from your peers next peer review?

*Portfolio*

Hand in the following: the process note, one copy of the publication draft, the concluding revision draft, the concluding planning note, peer responses, two mid-process drafts, two exploratory drafts, and any additional notes or responses having to do with the essay. I have already seen the response essays. Please carefully label all but the publication drafts—these will have titles and bylines. Use the order above, process note on top. When I hand these back, put all papers in your three-ring binder and return the folder to me.

*Criteria*
- A clear focus that organizes the conversation you are representing
- Clear explanations of the ideas in the published texts and your own responses and ideas
- Descriptive language that shows as well as tells information
- Transitions between paragraphs and between narrating, explaining, and interpreting
- Interpretations that make meaning of your ideas as well as the authors'
- Analyses that include dialogue with the authors' ideas
- Tone and style that invite dialogue and invite the authors to stand their ground even as you stand your own—the ability to say, "I see it differently/similarly," without dominating or capitulating
- Clear use of summaries, paraphrases, and quotes, including introducing and explaining each
- Process of revising—distinct changes between drafts
- Proofreading and proper MLA citation

## Essay 3: Representing the Tension Between the Individual and the Community

In this third essay, I invite you to explore the tension between individuals' needs and the needs of the communities to which those individuals belong. By needs, I mean basic human rights and values:

- Autonomy: the right to choose your own path
- Connection: the right to belong to groups whose values make sense to you
- Safety, food, shelter: the right to a life free from want
- Self-expression: the right to express one's self freely
- Justice: the right to fair and equal treatment

Communities also have needs or values that we learn as rules and guidelines for getting along and for doing work with one another collectively. Some of these rules grant rights to some people but not others. We first learn these at home (our primary socialization) and then at school and other institutions (our secondary socialization). Some of what we learn tells us who we are (our social identities: girl/boy, child/adult, black/white, poor/rich, etc.) and how we are valued and what we deserve. These rules also tell us who other people are and how they should be valued and what they deserve. In the process of learning these rules, we experience the tension between what we need as individuals (our rights that are unmet) and what our communities expect and need from us (the rules that either grant or deny us rights). We also witness how others' rights are often unmet.

This assignment guides you to explore this tension by contemplating how the rules or norms in your communities have granted or denied rights to you or someone close to you. We will begin by exploring social identities both experientially through class exercises and then through readings. This essay will give you a chance to tell your own story, to use the information you learn from the published essays, and to invite those who have represented you into a dialogue about the tension between the individual and the community.

*Exploratory Draft Begun in Class*
Arrange the dots on your shirt from most important—the identity that makes the most difference to you in your life or the identity you're most aware of—to the identity you're least aware of or makes the least difference to you. What do you notice? What might it mean?

gender = white
age = blue
occupation = yellow

race/ethnicity = red

other = green

Explore your own lived experiences with the following prompts. Describe a moment when

- you first realized you were a boy or a girl
- you first realized your own or your family members' sexual identities
- you first realized your own or your family members' ethnicities/races
- you first realized your own or your family members' economic classes
- you first realized your own or your family members' religions
- others assumed things about you that you thought were not true

Now that you've begun to story your lived experiences, pick the two stories that are most compelling for you; continue to story those experiences by explaining (writing) the realizations you had and what those stories/experiences meant to you then and now.

Write a story about a time when you realized that you or someone close to you was granted or denied rights based on your own or that person's social identity. Aim for as much sensory detail as possible: help your readers see, feel, and hear the experience, and use dialogue too.

### Dialogue Paper—500 Words for Peer Review

Read Bobbi Harro's "Cycle of Socialization." Take notes about the main ideas in Harro, and then, separately, take notes about your reactions: thoughts, associations, memories, and feelings. Type a reflection that states what you hear the author saying and the connections between the story you wrote in the exploratory draft and the reading. Then record which of your own reactions have or have not changed as you have moved through this assignment.

### Mid-process Draft: 1,000 Words Typed

Using what you've learned in peer reviews and readings, write a letter to a young person close to you and to a larger group about the story in the exploratory draft and your thoughts concerning the reading from the dialogue paper. Write the letter like a letter: include a greeting and personal details you share with the young person you are writing to. Write it like an essay also, with a clear purpose that invites the audience into a dialogue with you about the main issue at stake. What is the main issue underlying the story you tell? Imagine two audiences: one, a young person close to you, and the other, an audience of strangers who are in fact across the table from you. Imagine you care not only about the young person close to you but also about the strangers who may disagree with you or even hate you. Imagine writing to them as if you care about them the way you care about the young person. Even though you may violently disagree with this group of strangers, imagine that you are NOT willing to lose one person as a potential or actual friend/ally—find a way to be honest and clear, kind and direct. Include

- a visual image
- a reference from the readings that you think helps explain a point you are making
- an analogy or metaphor likening one object or event to another. For example, in her essay about herself as a writer, Linda Brodkey writes, "Writing was the girl's passport."

*Concluding Revision*
Revise your letter. Bring Diana Hacker, *A Writer's Reference,* and Joseph Trimmer, *Writing with Purpose,* to class for revising, editing, and proofreading.

*Portfolio*
Paper-clip to hand in the following:

- Final process note—a note addressed to Zan about writing this piece
- Final draft—use a title and a byline and have it proofread and signed by a person in class
- Typed peer reviews

Label all drafts and notes except the dialogue paper, which I will have. Use the order above, final process note on top.

### Criteria

- Descriptive language that evokes vivid images and tells as well as shows your story
- A clear point or focus
- Transitions between paragraphs
- Interpretations of your story that make meaning of your story
- Analyses that include a dialogue with the ideas in the reading
- Tone and style that invite dialogue with the audience
- A closing that proposes a future doable action
- Process of revising—distinct changes between drafts
- Proofreading—correct spelling and sentence structures

## Essay 4: Representing a Community Issue

In this project, you will be representing multiple aspects of a community issue. The purpose of this assignment is to give you an opportunity to learn about a particular issue—from your own primary research, published articles, and an agency—and invite us to seriously think about this issue. I ask you to present multiple points of view, including your own, and lay these views in front of us without moralistic judgment, instead pointing us to examine the feelings and the needs inherent in each viewpoint. We'll begin by simply reporting what we observe—what others are doing and saying about this issue—and then use analysis and interpretation to guess at the underlying feelings and needs of others. We'll work at separating out the underlying needs from the strategies and linking the strategies to values.

For example, if I am reading about a group that is protesting war with Iraq, I am guessing that nonviolence is a value they hold and that they disagree with the strategy of war to meet their need for safety. Further, they probably feel angry because they're telling themselves that those who advocate for the war are "inhuman and thoughtless" (moralistic judgments), and I can translate that into feelings of fear and needs for cooperation, consideration, and again, safety. I can also look for ways this group is trying to communicate their feelings and needs and for strategies they offer instead of war.

Aim at creating a conversation between these multiple viewpoints, keeping an eye on the humanness, the people behind those viewpoints, and invite us as readers into that conversation, lead us through it. Imagine you are able and willing not only to state your own feelings and needs around this issue but also to support others in stating their own feelings and needs, too. Work at learning with these others rather than attempt to dominate them or imagine they are dominating you. Try to hold in mind that you and the others each have pieces of the truth—corresponding to our social identities and histories—and none of us has the whole truth. Again, cultivate curiosity!

### Exploratory Draft Begun in Class

*The issue and guiding question.* Expect the question to change and evolve.

- What kinds or types of issues face communities?
- What are the different communities to which you belong on campus and at home?
- What kinds of issues are important in those communities?
- Of the above issues, which are most important to you or concern you the most?
- List five issues you would be willing to investigate and, if you know them, names of agencies you think might address these issues.

Choose two issues and recall situations for each in which that issue was somehow central—it might be a situation from your own life or one from a movie or book. Describe scenes, people involved, conversations, smells, tastes, noises, and other sensations. Write nonstop for as long as possible, striving to record as many vivid images and emotions as you can.

*Selecting an issue.* Now, pick one of those issues, write it at the top of a paper, and distribute it to ten of your classmates to gather research questions. Select a guiding question that is specific. Continue exploring what you know or don't know about this issue with the following questions:

- What have you observed people and yourself doing around this issue?
- What are you telling yourself about their actions, your actions, the issue?
- What are your feelings and needs regarding this issue?
- What do you know about this issue?
- What do you want to know about this issue?
- Who do you think this issue touches (name specific constituencies), and what are their feelings and needs in regard to this issue?

*Summary of published information.* Use your guiding question to find information at the library. Note in your binder the following when you find the citation: "Name of Article," *Name of Source,* number and volume (if it has one), page numbers of entire piece, call number, location of information in the library. Make a copy of the entire article or send it to yourself via e-mail.

Type up a summary of the information and copy down quotes from it that further explain, explore, or interpret some aspect of the issue you are exploring.

*Summary of agency due at conference.* Next, using the Internet, find an organization, an agency that addresses some aspect of this issue. Type up a summary of what you find out about how it addresses the issue, who it assists, and why. Look for a mission statement. Note in your binder the Internet address and the date the site was last updated as well as the date you visited.

*Survey workshop in class.* Finally, create a survey using your own research question as guidelines. Distribute the survey to at least ten people. Collect and review the completed surveys. Type up a summary of the results after you have tabulated them. What do you notice?

What do you think the results mean? Generate as many "I notice . . ." and "It might mean . . ." statements as you can. Be as specific as you can—note any direct quotes you think you might use in your essay.

*Pilot introduction.* Review the summaries and your answers to the exploratory questions and all the other information you've gathered, then set them aside. Write a pilot introduction using your guiding question. Be sure to include a strong narrative voice, an "I" that is you. Make a list of the rhetorical strategies you hope to use in your essay and an outline or map of your proposed essay.

### Mid-planning Note
Write a note to me and you about how you will create your mid-process draft.

### First Draft
Using your guiding question, organize your essay to address that question. In your essay, address how one media source represents this issue, how one agency deals with the issue, and how one population understands the issue. Write an essay that guides readers to understand not only the issue you're exploring but also why this issue is important to you and your community. Be sure to type this and use proper MLA citations, including a works cited section below the last paragraph of the essay. Include a strong narrative voice, yours. You will have a chance to do primary research and include this in your thinking about the issue in your concluding revision draft.

### Typed Peer Review Note
Type up the peer review session. Write a note that explains what you will do next—how will you revise your mid-process draft? Be sure to review the criteria and your peer review notes as you plan.

### Second Draft
Revise and document this piece to include the survey you've done. Be sure to use proper in-text and works cited entries and techniques. Represent this essay as a conversation between you and the sources you have created and found. Invite us to do something, to consider some aspect of the issue you are exploring. Create a clean, proofread copy for evaluation.

*Artistic Display*

Today we will also begin to plan how you will artistically present your paper gallery-style to our class. We will display the artistic version of the paper in class—you might use a collection of poems, a simple poster, a collage, a sculpture, the manuscript of a play, music lyrics, etc. Think of all the different ways artists use visual and musical art as well as the written word to communicate their ideas.

Using your plan to guide you, create a piece that will inform and move us, your audience. If you are writing a poem, consider beginning with images. If you are writing a song, perhaps think of a refrain. If you write something with characters in it, start with descriptions or sketches of those characters and ideas for scenes and places, and let the plot or action evolve from the characters. Use all your sources to transform your essay into a satisfying work of art.

*Process Note*

Use the criteria and explain how you met the criteria, what you are pleased with, and what you would revise if you had more time. Explain the changes you made between drafts and why. Tell me what was most challenging and what you learned doing this project as well as provide questions for me as a reader/evaluator.

*Portfolio*

Hand in, paper-clipped together, the process note; the proofread concluding revision draft as well as the beginning concluding revision draft; peer responses; the mid-process draft; the final, carefully cited and proofread exploratory draft and any additional notes or responses; and the pilot introduction. Please carefully label all but the publication draft; this will have a title. Use the order above, process note on top.

*Criteria*

- Clear theme that guides readers to explore and carefully consider your issue
- Descriptive language that shows as well as tells
- Distinct narrative voice
- Transitions between paragraphs
- Interpretations and analyses of the information you gathered and your own experiences

- Dialogue with the ideas in the sources
- Tone and style that invite dialogue, relationship, with the audience
- Closing that leaves the reader thinking—avoid trick endings or neatly wrapping things up
- Process of revising—distinct changes between drafts
- Proofreading and proper MLA citations for written version of your essay

## Essay 5: Representing Your Portfolio

This essay includes an in-depth review of each of your other essays, including specific references to your essays and to the letter about your essays from your partner as well as a future plan for yourself as a writer. It also includes an in-depth letter to your partner that carefully reviews each of your partner's essay. You will use the portfolio review essay to introduce a magazine, a portfolio of your work in this class. It will include publication drafts of each of your four essays as well as the letters between yourself and your partner.

### Peer Review Letter

We will begin this process in class. Give copies of your final drafts to your partner—someone you feel will be fair and kind with your work, someone with whom you feel comfortable.

Once you have received your partner's essays, do an in-depth review of each one. Review all the final drafts you've been given. Plan to write about a page for each:

- Say what the author was "doing" in the piece, and set that "doing" in a rhetorical context. For example, "As the author wrote this piece, he was reflecting on his beliefs about *x* and how they developed. The author was writing chiefly to understand what happened, but it seemed the author might also imagine that what he wrote would be read by classmates and maybe hoped it would encourage them to reflect on their own beliefs." Or, "The author was trying to invite other students into a dialogue about drug and alcohol use on campus—maybe the author could send this piece to the *Collegian* for publication." Or, "The author created a dialogue about oppression between herself and the three published authors apparently to better understand her own responsibility in relation to racism on this campus."

- Say what aspects of the piece you liked most or found most effective.
- Say what aspects you liked least and what changes you would suggest.
- Say how well the author met the criteria for each assignment (see assignment sheets).

Next, type an in-depth letter to the author discussing each of the essays and overall patterns you see in the author's development as a writer over the course of the semester. Be sure to use examples from the author's essays to illustrate your points. For example, when you address the question of how the author's ability to analyze and interpret has changed over the semester, be sure to show a "before and after" example from the essays. Another question you might ask and then use quotes or paraphrases from the essays to illustrate is, "How has the author's sense of audience changed?" Think of yourself as a coach as you evaluate and consider the author's work. Be careful to discuss both the strengths of this writer and this writer's growing edges, places where the author is working hard to improve. Strive for kindness, honesty, and constructive criticism. Describe what is effective and not so effective and why. Type and carefully edit this letter and save a copy for your own portfolio, then give a copy to your partner.

*Exploratory Draft*
Now it is your turn to evaluate your own essays, your own growth as a writer. Set aside the letter from your peer and use the same questions (above). Add to those questions these two:

- Say what changes you made between drafts of the essay and why. Be sure to refer to your process notes—they should have this information in them.
- Say what you learned or discovered about your writing or yourself through this piece.

*Mid-process Draft*

Begin this draft by reviewing your progress this semester. Go back and write a review of the range or "kinds" of writing you tried, your strengths/weaknesses as a writer, your most/least effective pieces, trends that you see in your work over time, characteristics that you see in your work independent of time. What trends do you see (analysis)? What do you think the trends mean (interpretation)?

Use your own in-depth analysis of the essays to write an extensive review of your essays in which you cite your own essays to make illustrations and points, and engage in analysis and interpretation of what you were doing and learning in each piece.

Write about your own future as a writer—a plan you may or may not end up following. This plan could include the kinds of writing you see yourself doing in the future, both academic and nonacademic. Will you build writing more deeply into your life? How many of your pieces would you like to publish, and where would you like to publish them or send them? How would you change the piece to give yourself the best chance possible for publication?

*Concluding Revision Draft*

Carefully organize and revise your mid-process draft using your partner's letter. Feel free at this point to meet with your partner and exchange peer reviews with one another. As you revise, include references to your partner's letter in your essay, citing it as you do so, to revise your in-depth analyses in particular and your overview and closing in general.

*Proofread Draft/Portfolio Publication*

You will be creating a small magazine, a portfolio, of the publication drafts of each final draft and the letters (one to you and one from you). Your portfolio review essay will serve as an introduction to your work. You will want to include a table of contents (please carefully number pages), a cover, and perhaps graphics that enhance your publication portfolio. Make two copies, one for me to keep and one for you to keep.

The product should be a stunningly edited (proofread every piece that goes into this magazine and submit all clean copies) and well-introduced publication, single-spaced. Make this a publication you can refer to for the rest of your life for ideas on how to compose various types of essays, notes (in the portfolio review essay) on what kind of drafting works best for you, and information on how to cite sources and how to proofread.

We will discuss your portfolio and your future plans as a writer.

*Criteria*
- Clear thesis about your writing and you as a writer
- Descriptive language that shows as well as tells
- Distinct and trustworthy voice narrating, explaining, analyzing, evaluating, and interpreting
- Transitions between paragraphs and between narrating, explaining, and interpreting
- Analyses that shows trends, patterns, similarities, and differences in your writing
- Interpretations that make meaning of the your essays, your writing process, and your relationship to writing
- Tone and style that invite dialogue, relationship, with the audience
- Clear use of summaries, paraphrases, and quotes from your essays and the letter, including introducing and explaining each
- Closing that proposes next steps
- Process of revising—distinct changes between drafts
- Proofreading, proper MLA citations, and works cited page
- Carefully designed publication including a cover, table of contents, and numbered pages

The portfolio publication is due at your scheduled final conference. This is your final. I will NOT accept late work, so please carefully plan and organize your time. Failure to submit a portfolio publication by the above time will result in your failure of the class. There are no exceptions. *Buena suerte*—good luck!

*The Deliberative Dialogue Forum Pamphlet*

This writing assignment asks you to collaborate with a group of other writers to address a campus community issue. We begin by issue-framing—settling on an issue to address and gathering the concerns people have about this issue, both here at the campus and on other campuses. The next step is to group the concerns into three or four categories and from there formulate a description of the issue—people's concerns—and at least three possible approaches to that issue.

In the forum pamphlet that your group drafts, you will describe the effect this issue has on communities and then detail at least three different approaches based on the concerns of three different segments of these communities. The forum pamphlet is meant to be used in a deliberative dialogue forum, a kind of conversation where people discuss together their own personal stakes in the issue and consider together the approaches presented from their own concerns. During the course of this deliberation, participants work hard at listening to and understanding concerns that are not their own. Although participants in the forum begin with three or four approaches, they also work to create other approaches that might work and satisfy all segments of the community.

Often communities decide they need more than one forum to address an issue. At the end of each forum, participants identify any ways in which their thinking has deepened or changed about the issue and then identify both common ground as well as differences that need to be discussed further.

*Group Work*
Answer the following questions individually:

- What kind of a group can you imagine working with to produce a collaboratively written project?
- What do you and each of the group members need to do in order to make the group work and produce a group project?

Once you have your answers, share them with two or three others and then decide together the two most important criteria you have for working with a group. Report these out to the class.

As a class, we'll decide on what sort of behaviors we need from one another in order to have the sort of groups with which we can work. We'll determine together what to do when a member of a group does not come through for the group. Finally, we will each willingly agree to use the guidelines for group work we have just created.

### Issue-Framing
Answer the following questions individually:

- What are the issues that concern you personally?
- What are the issues that concern those close to you?
- What are the issues that concern your hometown, neighborhood, or family?
- What are the issues that concern your state, national, or global community?

Share your top three issues, the ones that concern you the most, with two or three others. As a group, decide which two issues are most important to you. Report those issues out.

After we've heard the top two from each group, consider these issues in your small groups. Decide together the one issue that is most important to your group. Report that issue out.

Now, decide individually which of the top issues you would be willing to address.

### Constituents
- Who else besides you and your group might have concerns about this issue? List the constituents on campus.
- Decide who in your group will contact each constituency.
- Brainstorm together questions for surveys and interviews.
- Make a plan to try out these questions on friends first to determine if they really get to each constituent's concerns.

### You and the Issue
In order to know what you think about the issue and to be able to hear clearly when other people think differently about it, now is the time to inventory your own concerns.

- What do you know about the issue?

- What do you want to know about the issue?
- What are your feelings about the issue?
- What values, wants, or needs do your feelings indicate are important for you?

*Research*

Do your interviews and surveys. Next, go to the library and do the following assignment with your group.

*Today in the Library . . .*
Rotate roles.

- Firestarter facilitates group, involves all members, and gives direction.
- Reporter reads aloud and reports out to whole class.
- Secretary takes notes.

Decide which questions your group has generated to use at the library and add any new questions. Divide the questions among the members and attempt to answer the questions by locating the following sources:

- a library book or video
- an article you find on Academic Search Premier or ERIC (EBSCO host)
- an article you find on Newspaper Source (EBSCO host)
- an organization that attempts to address one aspect of the topic

Report out to the workshop one important aspect of your topic you learned today from one of the sources above or an important new question that was generated by your search.

Next, type your answers as a paragraph. Assign every person (including those absent) one of the sources above (individuals or pairs).

- What did you discover about the issue and people's concerns?
- What are your observations about the article/video/book/ Web site (describe words, tone, stories, quotes, examples used)?

- Who wrote or produced it, and what are your value judgments about the author?
- Who do you think the author sees as the audience?
- What background do you think the author imagines the audience shares?
- How do the audience and author feel about the topic, and how do you know?
- What are the needs or values and interests or concerns of this audience regarding the topic?
- What is the purpose of this piece? What does the author want the audience to do about the topic?
- How does this author perceive the topic? What is the author's approach?
- How do you perceive the topic after reading the piece?

### Concern Gathering

Concern gathering will involve a whole class discussion, one issue per class period. We'll go around the room, carefully listing the concerns on poster paper until we have thoroughly answered the question, "What are people's concerns about this issue?"

Next, we'll group the concerns by underlying beliefs, asking ourselves, "What are the values or beliefs underlying this concern?"

Once we have three or four groups, we'll work at formulating an approach from each group of concerns.

### Drafting

Finally, we are ready to begin to draft a forum pamphlet. First, we'll conduct analysis of another forum pamphlet to see how we might want to introduce and describe our issue and each of our approaches.

The audience for this forum is a group of students from a variety of backgrounds and beliefs. Your job is to invite them to see and understand the tensions in that issue and three distinct approaches to those tensions.

- Opening paragraphs and title should catch and keep the audience's attention.

- Description and background in opening paragraphs and approaches where you use vivid specifics should help the reader experience your issue and any important information he or she needs in order to understand the issue and approaches.
- Closing of the opening paragraphs should clearly introduce the tensions in the approaches.
- Approaches built on analysis and interpretation of the issue should be bulleted with each of the headings as in the "Sex" pamphlet.
- Documentation of the sources you researched need to be in MLA format for in-text citations.
- A works cited page of your sources should be provided; use the MLA format from Diana Hacker, *A Writer's Reference,* for in-text and works cited guidance.

*Peer Review of Pamphlet*

Read another group's pamphlet aloud. Write them a note that answers all the prompts below.

- Describe how the title and the opening paragraphs of the introduction keep or don't keep your attention. Make suggestions on improving it.
- Describe what specifics and background you read in the introduction. Is the information given in an unbiased way? If not, suggest how it might be less biased. Is the information clear? Describe ways to make it more clear. What other information do you need?
- What questions could the introduction close with to get readers to think about the approaches that follow?
- How could the titles and openings of each approach be more clear and attention-getting?
- What does the section on "Supporters Believe" need to make it more effective?
- What does the section on "What to Do" need—action steps? a description of programs or laws?
- What does the section on "Critics" need? Does it criticize the approach in a logical way?

• How does the "Trade-Offs" section describe what we lose if we go with this approach?

In your own groups, discuss revisions you'll make for Thursday. Use crayons to underline where the student authors are using their own words and where they are using someone else's. Add in-text citations where needed, and create a works cited page for all sources the group used.

*Criteria*
• Drafting and revision: substantial changes between drafts and notes
• Process notes from each member: detailed and specific
• Opening paragraphs and title that catch and keep the audience's attention
• Description and background in opening paragraphs and approaches where you use vivid specifics that help the reader experience your issue and any important information he or she needs in order to understand the issue and approaches
• Closing of the opening paragraphs that clearly introduces the tensions in the approaches
• Approaches built on analysis and interpretation of the issue, bulleted with each of the headings as in the "Sex" pamphlet
• Documentation of the sources you researched in MLA format for in-text citations
• A works cited page of your sources (use MLA format from Diana Hacker, *A Writer's Reference,* for in-text and works cited guidance)
• Proofreading that yields a nearly flawless draft in terms of grammar and punctuation (use standardized college English)

# Appendix B
## Guided Imagery

Find a comfortable position to sit in and let your eyes rest by closing them or focusing softly on the carpet or ceiling, anywhere you
can let them rest so that you can attend to your own inner world.
Select a moment in time from the memories you have just listed.

Hold that moment in mind. Put yourself back in that place.

Where are you?

What do you see?

What do you hear?

What do you smell?

What do you taste?

What sensations do you have in your body, and where are those
sensations?

What do you feel and where in your body are those feelings?

What is the expression on your face?

What are you wearing?

What time of day is it?

What is the weather like?

What season is it?

What are you saying or not saying?

What are you thinking? Is it the same or different from what
you're saying?

Who else is there with you?

What do they look like?

What are the expressions on their faces?

What feelings are they expressing?

What are they saying or not saying?

What do you think they are thinking?

What is happening? Who is doing or not doing what?

Take a last look around, soaking in all the sights, smells, sensations, noises—every detail. Now, open your eyes and begin writing nonstop for ten minutes.

Finish what you are writing and describe what you were going to write next so that you can pick up where you left off. Try using this writing in your draft, or pick another scenario and do this guided imagery with it and use that in your draft.

# Appendix C
## Grading Contract for College Writing

In this writing class, you are asked to inhabit two roles—that of a writer in a writing community and that of a student at the university.

In a writing community, grades do not exist. Everyone writes, everyone shares, everyone offers feedback, everyone revises. Everyone writes the best piece possible without worrying if this particular teacher will give it an A. Sometimes we write really good stuff, and sometimes we write not-so-great stuff. Sometimes we need to write a lot of bad stuff before we know exactly what it is we want to say and what we think. Writing is also a series of plateaus and peaks. It seems like we write the same for a while, and then suddenly our writing improves dramatically, and then we plateau for a while. Sometimes our first couple of essays are okay, but then we make a dramatic improvement in the third and fourth.

Grades do exist and play a large role in your lives as members of the university community. Grades are the currency we use here. Grades determine if you can stay in school, if you are eligible for scholarships and financial aid, if you will be admitted into your major or graduate school. There is a great deal of pressure for everyone to do well and get good grades.

Being a writer in a writing community and being a student in a class at the university may seem to be in conflict with one another. In order to grow and develop as writers, we need to be able to take risks in our writing, to sometimes fail, to try out different strategies, different voices. As members of the university community, we need to think about grades—as students you need to earn a grade in order to receive credit for this course, and I, as the teacher, need to assign a grade that reflects the work and progress you made over the course of the semester.

The use of this grading contract attempts to reconcile this conflict by removing some of the anxiety we all feel about grades; what follows is an outline of the things you need to do in order to earn a specific grade. The assumption is that everyone wants to earn at least a passing grade of C. However, for the majority of us, a passing grade is really just not good enough. We want to do well—to earn at least a B or higher. Outlined below is what you will need to do in order to earn the particular grade you want to earn.

It is important to keep in mind that this course is based on the assumption that writing is a process and that in order to grow and to develop as a writer, you need to go through all the steps of the writing process. The process you go through does lead to a final product— the final draft of your essay. This leads to another conflict—product vs. process. Sometimes you may put a great deal of effort into each draft of an essay, and your final draft still needs work. You may take a big risk with an essay, attempting to write in a way that you have never written before, but in the end it just doesn't work very well. And sometimes you may produce the best piece of writing you have ever written in the first draft. This grading contract attempts to reconcile this conflict by taking into account the quality of the final draft of each essay as well as the process you went through in writing it. As you will see below, faithfully going through the process for each essay and completing all the required work for the course will enable you to pass the course with a C. To earn a grade higher than a C, the quality of your work begins to factor in. How well you go through the process of each essay, the quality of the final draft, and the effort you demonstrate in completing all the requirements of the course will enable you to earn a higher grade.

In other words, the contract can take you only so far. As the teacher in this course, I have the job and responsibility to create a space that enables you to not only write but also expand, explore, and develop your writing skills. As the students in this course, it is up to you to use this space. Those of you who use the space as outlined in the syllabus will pass the course. Honors grades are reserved for those who use the space to push the limits of their own writing, to expand, explore, and develop their writing skills, to take risks and to succeed.

I realize that some of this may sound a little vague. Your final grade is not meant to be a surprise. Although I won't be assigning letter grades to the final drafts of your essays or to anything else you write all semester, I will provide you with feedback to guide you along the way and to let you know how you are doing. On the drafts of your essays, peer review and our conferences will be geared toward revision, hopefully enabling you to write the best essay you possibly can. On the final draft of each essay, my comments will focus on how successfully you worked through the process and on what you might do to revise that final draft, if you so choose. I will also use a check system to help you keep track of your progress. A check-minus will indicate that you fell below the minimum requirements for the essay, a check will indicate that you met the minimum requirements, and a check-plus will indicate that you exceeded the requirements.

It is important to remember that your final grade does not rely solely on the process and the writing you do for your major essays. The checks you receive on your essays indicate how well you are doing for the essay portion that makes up your final grade. In order to grow and to develop as a writer, it is also important that you experience and explore different ways of writing—private writing, process writing, etc. It is also important that you be a supportive and contributing member of our writing community.

For each of the five essays, put a good faith effort into each draft. By "good faith" I mean following the guidelines on each essay assignment sheet, including the word count. Each assignment sheet provides a list of criteria against which you and I will evaluate each essay.

*Process Writing*
I require a good faith effort on all the notes about your writing process.

*Peer Workshops*
Giving and receiving feedback is essential. As a giver, frame your suggestions specifically and concretely. For example: "I was lost reading paragraph 2. Could you explain to me what you meant there?"

As a receiver, ask for specific and concrete feedback. For example: "I'm struggling with the end—I want to leave the reader with a question to consider. Can you help me come up with one?"

As a speaker, take responsibility for your opinions: "I'm angry about what you just said because . . ."

As a listener, reflect back on what the speaker said if you need clarity: "So, you're mad that I support campaign finance reform because you want less rules?"

*Journal*
I require a good faith effort and three binder pages per week, front and back, to be counted in class once a week. Three gets you a ✓, less than that a ✓-, and more than that a ✓+.

*Shorter In-/Out-of-Class Assignments and Activities*
I require a good faith effort.

*Writing Community Member*
Regular attendance is essential—the class works best when everyone is here, on time, and prepared. More than two absences for any reason during the semester affects our work together and your grade.

*Participation*
A good faith effort is required in all activities and class discussions, especially respecting the viewpoints and perspectives of everyone in class as well as those of the published authors we read. See guidelines on peer workshops for tips on respectfully responding.

This grading grid will help both you and me see what grade you are earning at any point in the semester. There is no extra credit in this course, though you may revise any essay by making an appointment with me to set a due date for the revised draft. There are no make-ups for missed in-class assignments. (Adapted from Professor Peggy Woods's college writing class, University of Massachusetts at Amherst)

Grading Grid

|  | C | C+/B- | B/B+ | A- | A |
|---|---|---|---|---|---|
| Overall late/missing/absent | 6 | 5 | 3–4 | 2 | 2 |
| 5 essays | 3 late drafts check on all essays | 2 late drafts check on all essays | 2 late drafts check on 3–5 essays check-plus on 1–2 essays | 1 late draft check on 2–3 essays check-plus on 2–3 essays | 1 late draft check on 1–2 essays check-plus on 3–4 essays |
| Process notes | 2 late/missing | 2 late/missing | 2 late/missing | 1 late/missing | 1 late/missing |
| Workshops (classes) | miss 5 | miss 3 | miss 3 | miss 2 | miss 2 |
| Journal | meet minimum | meet minimum | exceed limit for 2–4 weeks | exceed limit for 4–6 weeks | exceed limit for 6–8 weeks |
| Other assignments | 2 late 2 missing | 2 late 2 missing | 2 late/missing | 1 late/missing | 1 late/missing |

# Notes

1. The names of speakers used in this book are pseudonyms.

2. Mollie Blackburn discusses a similar phenomenon in her article "Exploring Literacy Performances and Power Dynamics at The Loft: Queer Youth Reading the World and the Word." The Loft, a GLBT community center by and for youth, also had a speaker's bureau composed of youth members. Blackburn studied literacy performances of speakers in their educational outreach project, a project much like UMass at Amherst's Speaker's Bureau. She also studied the tension between youth speakers on the bureau and youth at the center who were not on the bureau. What she notes is how this tension at times resulted in literacy performances on the bureau that challenged and transformed inequitable power dynamics. At other times, what speakers on the bureau said reinforced and replicated inequalities, particularly between those who identified as gay, lesbian, or bisexual and those who identified as transgendered.

3. See the last chapter where I address social identity development through Bobbi Harro's article "The Cycle of Socialization."

4. The first DOMA, signed into law by President Clinton in September 1996, required the federal government to ignore legal marriages between same-sex couples and allowed states to ignore such marriages performed in any other state. The DOMA "violates the Full Faith and Credit Clause of the Constitution (Article IV, Section 1), which provides that the court judgments of one state shall be recognized as valid in other states" *(Consultants on Religious Tolerance)*. In turn, the DOMA denies the Constitutional "right to travel, temporarily or permanently from state to state," for those same-sex couples married, for example, in Massachusetts who travel to Rhode Island. The new definition of marriage as

> between one man and one woman . . . has the effect of treating all lesbian and gay couples as strangers under Federal laws, denying them such basic considerations as: bereavement or sick leave . . . pension or social security continuation . . . joint tax returns and exemptions . . . on estate taxes . . . veteran's discounts . . . [and] immigration and residency for partners from other countries.

In addition, the DOMA "violates the Fifth Amendment guarantee of equal protection" *(Consultants on Religious Tolerance)*. By stipulating that people must be married to enjoy certain rights and privileges and then denying same-sex partners the ability to legally marry, the federal government creates second-class citizen status for gay and lesbian couples.

5. My adviser, Anne Herrington, helped me to see this.

6. I am also indebted to psychologist Marshall Rosenberg's philosophy and practice of nonviolent communication, which is in turn based on Gandhi's concept of nonviolence or *satyagraha,* defined in his words as "the force which is born of truth and love" (86). According to Gandhi, we as human beings can never be entirely free of what he calls "the deadly coil of *himsa* (the destruction of life)" because living necessarily involves violence; however, human beings can be true to the practice of nonviolence if we consistently strive to take action from a place of self-restraint and compassion for all beings, bearing in mind we are each connected to every other being on the planet.

# Works Cited

Bacon, Nora. "The Trouble with Transfer: Lessons from a Study of Community Service Writing." *Michigan Journal of Community Service Learning* 6 (Fall 1999): 53–62.

Banks, William P. "Written Through the Body: Disruptions and 'Personal' Writing." *College English* 66.1 (Sept. 2003): 21–40.

Bartholomae, David, and Anthony R. Petrosky. *Facts, Artifacts, and Counterfacts: Theory and Method for a Reading and Writing Course.* Upper Montclair, NJ: Boynton/Cook, 1986.

Blackburn, Molly. "Exploring Literacy Performances and Power Dynamics at The Loft: Queer Youth Reading the World and the Word." *Research in the Teaching of English* 37 (May 2003): 467–91.

Bridwell-Bowles, Lillian. "Discourse and Diversity: Experimental Writing in the Academy." *College Composition and Communication* 43 (1992): 349–68.

Brodkey, Linda. "Articulating Poststructural Theory in Research on Literacy." *Multi-Disciplinary Perspectives on Literacy Research.* Ed. Richard Beach et al. Urbana, IL: NCTE, 1992. 2–23.

———. "On the Subject of Class and Gender in 'The Literacy Letters.'" *College English* 51.2 (Feb. 1989): 125–41.

———. "Writing on the Bias." *Writing Permitted in Designated Areas Only.* Minneapolis: U of Minnesota P, 1996. 29–31.

Brooke, Robert E. "Underlife and Writing Instruction." *College Composition and Communication* 38.2 (May 1987): 141–53.

———. *Writing and Sense of Self: Identity Negotiation in Writing Workshops.* Urbana, IL: NCTE, 1991.

Burke, Kenneth. *A Grammar of Motives.* 1945. Berkeley: University of California Press, 1969.

———. *A Rhetoric of Motives.* 1950. Berkeley: University of California Press, 1969.

Butler, Judith. *Gender Trouble: Feminism and the Subversion of Identity.* New York: Routledge, 1990.

Chiseri-Strater, Elizabeth. *Academic Literacies: The Public and Private Discourse of University Students.* Portsmouth, NH: Boynton/Cook, 1991.

Clare, Eli. "The Mountain." Curtis et al. 71–80.

*Consultants on Religious Tolerance.* "Prohibiting Same-Sex Marriage in the U.S.: Federal and State 'DOMA' Legislation." May 14, 2005. June 24, 2005 <http://www.religioustolerance.org>.

Curtis, Marcia, et al. *The Original Text-Wrestling Book*. Dubuque, IA: Kendall/ Hunt, 2001.

Deans, Thomas. *Writing and Community Action: A Service-Learning Rhetoric with Readings*. New York: Addison, 2003.

———. *Writing Partnerships: Service-Learning in Composition*. Urbana, IL: NCTE, 2000.

Deans, Thomas, and Zan Gonçalves. "Writing Out of Bounds: Service-Learning Projects in the Composition Classroom and Across the Curriculum." *College Teaching* 46.1 (Winter 1998): 15–18.

Elbow, Peter. Foreword. Curtis et al. 1–4.

Flower, Linda. *Problem-Solving Strategies for Writing in College and Community*. Fort Worth: Harcourt, 1998.

Fox, Thomas. "Basic Writing as Cultural Conflict." *Journal of Education* 172 (1990): 65–83.

———. *The Social Uses of Writing: Politics and Pedagogy*. Norwood, NJ: Ablex, 1990.

Frank, Thomas. "Why Johnny Can't Dissent." Curtis et al. 111–21.

Freire, Paulo. *Pedagogy of the Oppressed*. Trans. Myra Ramos. New York: Routledge, 1994.

Gandhi. *The Penguin Gandhi Reader*. Ed. Rudrangshu Mukherjee. New York: Penguin, 1996.

Hacker, Diana. *A Writer's Reference*. Boston: Bedford/St. Martin's, 2003.

Hardiman, Rita, and Bailey Jackson. "Conceptual Foundations for Social Justice Courses." Curtis et al. 156–68.

Harro, Bobbie. "The Cycle of Socialization." Curtis et al. 169–78.

Herrington, Anne, and Marcia Curtis. *Persons in Process: Four Stories of Writing and Personal Development in College*. Urbana, IL: NCTE, 2000.

Hindman, Jane. "Making Writing Matter: Using 'the Personal' to Recover(y) and Essential(ist) Tension in Academic Discourse." *College English* 64.1 (Sept. 2001): 88–108.

*Human Rights Campaign*. "HRC Marriage Center." 2004. June 24, 2005 <http:// www.hrc.org>.

Lyons, Scott. "Rhetorical Sovereignty: What Do American Indians Want from Writing?" *College Composition and Communication* 51.3 (Feb. 2000): 447–68.

Malinowitz, Harriet. *Textual Orientations: Lesbian and Gay Students and the Making of Discourse Communities*. Portsmouth, NH: Boynton/Cook, 1995.

Moss, Beverly J. "Ethnography and Composition: Studying Language at Home." *Methods and Methodology in Composition Research*. Ed. Gesa Kirsch and Patricia A. Sullivan. Carbondale: Southern Illinois UP, 1992. 153–71.

Newkirk, Thomas. *The Performance of Self in Student Writing*. Portsmouth, NH: Boynton/Cook, 1997.

O'Reilly, Mary Rose. *The Peaceable Classroom*. Portsmouth, NH: Boynton/Cook, 1993.

Phelan, Shane. *Getting Specific: Postmodern Lesbian Politics.* Minneapolis: U of Minnesota P, 1994.

Powell, Malea. "Rhetorics of Survivance: How American Indians Use Writing." *College Composition and Communication* 43 (Feb. 2002): 396–434.

Prior, Paul. "Literate Activity and Disciplinarity: The Heterogeneous (Re)Production of American Studies Around a Graduate Seminar." *Mind, Culture, and Activity* 4.4 (1997): 275–97.

———. "Response, Revision, Disciplinarity: A Microhistory of a Dissertation Prospectus in Sociology." *Written Communication* 11.4 (1994): 483–533.

———. *Writing/Disciplinarity: A Sociohistorical Account of Literate Activity in the Academy.* Mahway, NJ: Erlbaum, 1998.

Ratcliffe, Krista. "Rhetorical Listening: A Trope for Interpretive Invention and a 'Code of Cross-Cultural Conduct.'" *College Composition and Communication* 51.2 (Dec. 1999): 195–224.

Rich, Adrienne. "Compulsory Heterosexuality and Lesbian Experience." *Adrienne Rich's Poetry and Prose.* Ed. Barbara Charlesworth Gelpi and Albert Gelpi. New York: Norton, 1993. 203–24.

Rosenberg, Marshall. *Nonviolent Communication . . . A Language of Compassion.* 8th ed. Encinitas, CA: Puddle Dancer, 2002.

Skolfield, Karen. "Exploring and Celebrating Voice in Gay, Lesbian, and Bisexual Writing Class." Conference on College Composition and Communication. Chicago. Mar. 1998.

*Speaker's Bureau Manual.* Amherst: Stonewall Center, U of Massachusetts, Fall 1996.

Spigelman, Candace. "Argument and Evidence in the Case of the Personal." *College English* 64.1 (Sept. 2001): 63–87.

Trimmer, Joseph. *Writing with Purpose.* 14th ed. New York: Houghton Mifflin, 2004.

University of Massachusetts at Amherst Center for Institutional Research. *Student Affairs Research.* Amherst: U of Massachusetts, 1993.

———. *Project Pulse.* Amherst: U of Massachusetts, 1993.

Wallace, David L. "Out in the Academy: Heterosexism, Invisibility, and Double Consciousness." *College English* 65.1 (Sept. 2002): 53–66.

Young, Morris. "Standard English and Student Bodies: Institutionalizing Race and Literacy in Hawaii." *College English* 64.4 (Mar. 2002): 405–31.

# Index

ZAN MEYER GONÇALVES is an assistant professor at Franklin Pierce College in Rindge, New Hampshire, where she teaches first-year composition and the first-year seminar with a focus on community issues and deliberation. She has published and given papers on community service learning and the use of deliberative dialogue in the classroom.

*Studies in Writing & Rhetoric*

In 1980 the Conference on College Composition and Communication established the Studies in Writing & Rhetoric (SWR) series as a forum for monograph-length arguments or presentations that engage general compositionists. SWR encourages extended essays or research reports addressing any issue in composition and rhetoric from any theoretical or research perspective as long as the general significance to the field is clear. Previous SWR publications serve as models for prospective authors; in addition, contributors may propose alternate formats and agendas that inform or extend the field's current debates.

SWR is particularly interested in projects that connect the specific research site or theoretical framework to contemporary classroom and institutional contexts of direct concern to compositionists across the nation. Such connections may come from several approaches, including cultural, theoretical, field-based, gendered, historical, and interdisciplinary. SWR especially encourages monographs by scholars early in their careers, by established scholars who wish to share an insight or exhortation with the field, and by scholars of color.

The SWR series editor and editorial board members are committed to working closely with prospective authors and offering significant developmental advice for encouraged manuscripts and prospectuses. Editorships rotate every five years. Prospective authors intending to submit a prospectus during the 1997 to 2002 editorial appointment should obtain submission guidelines from Robert Brooke, SWR editor, University of Nebraska-Lincoln, Department of English, P.O. Box 880337, 202 Andrews Hall, Lincoln, NE 68588-0337.

General inquiries may also be addressed to Sponsoring Editor, Studies in Writing & Rhetoric, Southern Illinois University Press, P.O. Box 3697, Carbondale, IL 62902-3697.